ST*A*

Your
New
Life

PRABIN SHARMA

*How to Stop Over thinking, Face Life Challenges, Take
Powerful Actions and Transform Yourself*

First Edition 14 April 2023
ISBN: B0BQ8PR5PL (ASIN)
ISBN - Paperback: 9798369894835

Independently Published by Prabin Sharma

Website: **www.prabinsharma.com**, For more information, email: connect@prabinsharma.com

Disclaimer

While all attempts have been made to verify the information provided in this publication, neither the author nor the publisher assumes any responsibility for errors, omissions, or contrary interpretations of the subject matter herein. This book is for entertainment purposes only. The views expressed are those of the author alone, and should not be taken as expert instruction or commands. The reader is responsible for his or her own actions. Adherence to all applicable laws and regulations, including international, federal, state, and local governing professional licensing, business practices, advertising, and all other aspects of doing business in the US, Canada, or any other jurisdiction is the sole responsibility of the purchaser or reader. Neither the author nor the publisher assumes any responsibility or liability whatsoever on the behalf of the purchaser or reader of these materials. Any perceived slight of any individual or organization is purely unintentional.

Table of Contents

Disclaimer i

Table of Contents.................................... ii

Dedication... iv

Epigraph... v

INTRODUCTION: Do not Skip it!............................ vi

Special Note: xi

Chapter 1: What is your new life? 1

Key Takeaways - 1 7

Chapter 2: How do you START your new life? 8

Key Takeaways - 2 23

Chapter 3: My START formula 24

Key Takeaways - 3 28

Chapter 4: S=Stop over thinking 29

4.1 What is over thinking? 29

4.2 Why is over thinking dangerous?..........33

4.3 Why do you over think? 37

4.4 How to stop over thinking?.....................41

Key Takeaways - 4 47

Chapter 5: T=Take care of Your Health 48

5.1 Importance of Holistic health.................48

5.2 Powerful Healthy Habits 55

5.3 Must Do smart ways of holistic health .61

Key Takeaways - 5.................................*68*

Chapter 6: A=Action is the Key................*69*

6.1 Action is the key to start your new life .69

6.2 Obstacles in taking actions 73

6.3 8 Ways to overcome procrastination ...76

Key Takeaways - 6.................................*80*

Chapter 7: R=Read *81*

7.1 Why do you read?......................................81

7.2 How to read 100 books in a year?..........86

7.3 *5 Ways to get the most out of any book*
....*90*

Key Takeaways - 7.................................*94*

Chapter 8: T=Teach What You Know.........*95*

8.1 Why should you teach?............................95

8.2 How will you teach? 99

Key Takeaways - 8...............................*104*

CONCLUSION.......................................*105*

Acknowledgment *106*

Gratitude: Request to Readers.............*107*

About the Author *108*

Upcoming Book of the Author *109*

Also By the Author *111*

Dedication

I dedicate this book to you, the readers who inspire and love me.

My Baba (father) who gives freedom to choose and follow the intuition in my life.

My mother who has always been my critics and my well-wisher.

Epigraph

CHAPTER 14, VERSE 19

[Shrimad Bhagavad-Gita]

"Nannyam gunebhyah kartaram yada
drastanupasyati,
Gunebhyasch param vetti madbhavam
so'dhigacchati."

(When wise persons see that in all work there is
no agent of action other than the three Gunas,
and they know Me to be transcendental to these
Gunas, they attain My divine nature.)

INTRODUCTION: Do not Skip it!

****

> *"There are worse crimes than burning books. One of them is not reading them."*
>
> *- Joseph Brodsky*

Do you want success? No.

Do you want happiness? No.

Do you want money? No.

Do you want to love? No.

What do you really want? Think a little.

You may seem busy to find happiness, to accumulate money, to love yourself or someone or try hard to accomplish something, but your fate decides more in your life than you do.

Is it your true nature? Never.

If you analyse the life span of a common person, you will find life runs its own way, creating many unfulfilled dreams. Let me share an interesting short story about the creation of human beings that you may hear or read.

God created the donkey, instructing it to carry everyone's burden and live for 40 years.

The donkey protested, asking for a reduced lifespan of 30 years, and God granted its wish.

God created the dog and required it to look after people's belongings, eat whatever it was given, and live for 40 years. The dog requested only 20 years, and God obliged it.

Next, God created the monkey and asked it to entertain with its tricks for 40 years.

The monkey petitioned for 30 years, and God agreed.

God created man at last and said to him, "You will be the greatest creature of all and live for 20 years. I give you the power to accomplish all your dreams, and bless you with the time to make a real difference in the world."

The man said, "20 years is a significant amount of time to make a lasting impact, but I know I can do more." He further added, asking for the ten years that the donkey had declined, the twenty years that the dog had refused, and the ten years that the monkey had rejected, "Grant me more 40 years, and I will show you what I am capable of."

Finally, God granted his wish. From then on, a man lived for sixty years. From infancy to adulthood, a person may spend 20 years as a blessed human, 10 years as a beast of burden to establish career and to marry, 20 years as a loyal guardian to rear members of a family, and 10 years as a playful entertainer for grandsons and others. Nevertheless, if that person does not take the time to savour the moments, no amount of time will ever be enough.

What is your take away from this story?

The most tragic reality of life is that many of us never truly understand the beauty of life; instead, many of us simply meander through existence, never appreciating the richness of experience.

It is a tragic truth that many people spend their days so busy planning for the future that they never get to enjoy the present. You may also rush through your days, weeks, and months without taking the time to value the richness of your experience and your hidden potential.

Life's beauty is a bittersweet experience.

What do you really want in your life?

Now, think awhile again.

I am sure you will agree with me. *Life transformation is what you desire.* You wish to become a different version of yourself. Your need is to add different colours to your life. You hope to change your monotonous life. *You want to start your new life.*

It happens with everyone. You want to do one thing, and you end up doing different things. Sometimes you delay taking the required steps to transform your life or you procrastinate very often. You think repeatedly very often. At last, everything goes in vain.

Pause. Take a deep breath. Now exhale.

Do you suffer from over thinking?

Can you often not implement your lessons?

Are you feeling stuck, anxious, or unmotivated?

Are you often overwhelmed by life's challenges?

Do you want to take control of your life and transform yourself?

If so, this book, **START Your New Life**: *How to Stop Over thinking, Face Life Challenges, Take Powerful Actions and Transform Yourself;* is for you.

This book will teach you how to change your mind-set, break through self-sabotaging habits and patterns, and start taking powerful steps towards transforming your life. You will learn essential techniques for managing anxiety and stress, building a positive attitude and self-confidence, and overcoming fear.

With this book, you will gain the knowledge and skills *necessary to start a new life* and create the life you truly desire. Reading this book will reveal to you the secrets of overcoming negative thinking and fears, discovering the power of personal transformation, and leading an extraordinary life.

With this systematic guide, you will learn how to break through the limiting beliefs you have about yourselves and the world, move beyond fear and stagnation, and develop an action-oriented mind-set. Through practical exercises, thought-provoking questions, and inspiring stories, you will gain the skills, courage, and confidence to create the life of your dreams. This book will be an essential resource for anyone who is ready to change his or her life.

Do not overthink. Over thinking can lead to life paralysis, lack of motivation, and depression. However, you do not have to be stuck in a cycle of negative thoughts. This book will teach you how to move beyond your fears and into a new way of living. Read this book; and it will encourage you to develop a positive outlook, learn to take risks, manage stress, and ultimately start a journey of self-discovery.

Congratulations to you as you have picked up your copy of this book and it shows that you are ready to take the next step and *start your new life*. Remember, this book is the key to unlocking a life of happiness, fulfilment, and joy.

With love and gratitude,

Good luck!

Special Note:

1. My endeavour is not to preach or to advocate my views, but to express my perspective only. I do not force readers to consider my perspective as a universal truth. As a reader, you are free to follow your heart. I share here my experiences, learnings and results to help you get similar outcomes and enjoy your life.

The publisher and the author make no guarantees concerning the level of success you may experience by following the advice and strategies in this book.
Moreover, you accept the risk that results will differ for each individual. The testimonials and examples provided in this book show exceptional results, which may not apply to the average reader and are not intended to represent or guarantee that you will achieve the same or similar results.

2. Unless otherwise showed; all the names, characters, businesses, places, events and incidents in this book are the product of the author's imagination or used fictitiously. Any resemblance to actual persons, living or dead, or actual events is coincidental.

3. I am not a doctor and this book is not medical advice. It contains thoughts, suggestions, and information that I used myself and I hope that may help you, but please seek medical advice for your condition and stop following my advice if you feel any uncomfortable situation following any health-related advice given in this book.

Chapter 1: What is your new life?

You have the power to control your own lives and create a happy future for yourselves and those around you. *What do you need?* You just need to decide to take charge and steer your lives in a positive direction. Even when you face difficulties, you can overcome them and turn your negative thoughts into positive ones. By reminding yourselves every day that you are in control, you become stronger, more confident, and more determined to succeed. All these can happen only if you start your new life.

What is your new life?

If you start your new life, it means it is a demonstration of your willingness to take responsibility for your actions and create a more beneficial and meaningful life experience. It is a chance to abandon old behaviors, thought patterns, and habits that are no longer helpful and replace them with those that will bring greater satisfaction.

This book focuses on *transforming your life* and makes you able to live the life of your dream. Beginning afresh is a sign of readiness to accept potential improvements. By reflecting on past mistakes, new beginnings open a path to success for the future.

Are you ready to face all of life's challenges head on?

Are you ready to take powerful, decisive action?

Starting your new life *means* taking control of your life, developing a growth mindset, building a brighter future, and transforms yourself. It is a deliberate decision to progress with courage and resolve, to establish a more meaningful life for oneself.

Have you read or heard about the parable of the Chinese bamboo tree?

It is a story that speaks to the human potential that we all possess.

Once upon a time, there lived a farmer. He was overwhelmed by the tribulations of life and he always felt disheartened by his failures. He decided to leave it all behind and hideaway in the woods. There, he encountered a hermit who asked him, "Why do you want to give up?"

The framer replied that he had lost all hope.

The hermit said, "Life can be overwhelming at times, and it's easy to get disheartened by our failures."

Then he handed over some seeds of bamboo trees to him and instructed to grow them. He was told that if he planted the seed, it would grow to be large and strong. The farmer came back to his home and planted a seed with care and hope, but for five years, nothing happened. The farmer faithfully watered and tended the soil, but no growth was visible.

He doubted the potential of his tree and even considered giving up. However, in the sixth year, the farmer looked at the seed and noticed something strange. The seed was cracking, almost as if something was pushing from within. He continued to water it and care for it, and sure enough, the seed sprouted.

This sudden growth amazed and encouraged the farmer. He soon noticed that the tree was growing faster. In only five weeks, the tree had grown to a staggering height of 80 feet. The farmer was astonished and amazed. He watched the tree grow and marveled at its strength and majesty.

He soon realized that the bamboo tree had been a symbol of hope for him. He visited the hermit once again and said, "That's amazing! It takes years of effort to water and nurture it, but nothing seems to happen until the fifth year - and then it grows an 80 feet tall in months!"

The hermit explained, *"The strength of the tree is because of the strong roots it has developed during the years of growth."*

He reminded the man that, during his struggles, he too had been growing strong roots of knowledge and resilience. That inspired the man. The man accepted that hard work and perseverance were necessary.

This parable speaks to the importance of having faith and perseverance in order to reach your full potential. It is only with patience and dedication that you can truly reach the heights that you are capable of. You must put in the hard work and dedication, even when the results may not be immediately visible. *Growth is a process*, and it takes time before you can see the results of your efforts.

Before you start your new life, I would like to make you familiar with the power of affirmation. If you practice and trust potential behind affirmations, you will harness amazing life transforming outcomes. Let me share here a little about affirmations.

What is affirmation?

Affirmation is a practice of speaking positive words to oneself, intending to reshape one's beliefs and actions.

Using affirmations has had transformative effects on one's life; from enabling one to overcome self-limiting beliefs, to helping one achieve their goals, and ultimately leading to a life of fulfillment and satisfaction.

Affirmations can seem simple, but they are a powerful tool that helps shift one's mindset towards positive thinking, which can help to build confidence and create self-fulfilling prophecies.

Why do I suggest you practice affirmations?

There are several reasons for that. Here is my top 10 reasons that force me to suggest that you practice them:

1. Affirmations improve your brain and alter your negative thought patterns.

2. Positive affirmations can improve your self-esteem and confidence levels.

3. Affirmations can help you let go of past traumas and move forward.

4. By practicing affirmations, you can attract positive people and experiences into your life.

5. Affirmations can help you release fear and anxiety and live a more peaceful life.

6. Affirmations can help you focus on your goals and achieve them more easily.

7. By repeating affirmations, you can train your mind to think positively and attract abundance.

8. Affirmations can help you accept and love yourself, which is essential for a happy life.

9. By regularly practicing affirmations, you can create a new reality for yourself.

10. Affirmations can help you live the life you truly want and deserve.

In conclusion, *affirmation can help you build a new life*.

Remember, it takes time and commitment to develop a practice of affirmations, but the benefits are worthwhile. By incorporating affirmations into your daily routine, you can start your new life. Practice them daily.

Here are *five* affirmations for you to start your new life.

Affirmation to Start Your New Life

1. _I embrace the power to create my future and accept accountability for my life._

2. _I am the sole authority of my happiness._

3. _I choose to concentrate on the positive aspects of life and am open to new prospects._

4. _I trust my capacity to make decisions that are valuable to me._

5. _I am unwavering in my conviction to realize my potential._

Remember, the act of starting your new life and incorporating affirmations to realize your desired outcomes can transform your life.

Affirmations have the potential to alter one's mindset and convictions, enabling one to recognize the potentialities and prospects in life. Through regular repetition of affirmative statements, one can reprogram the subconscious mind and manifest the existence one seeks. It is essential to bear in mind that your own thoughts and ideas shape your reality.

***

Key Takeaways - 1

1. To start your new life is your willingness to take responsibility for your actions and create a more beneficial and meaningful life experience.

2. Starting your new life *means* taking control of your life, developing a growth mindset, building a brighter future, and transforms yourself.

3. To start your new life is a deliberate decision to progress with courage and resolve, to establish a more meaningful life for oneself.

4. *Growth is a process*, and it takes time before you can see the results of your efforts.

5. Affirmation is a practice of speaking positive words to oneself, intending to reshape one's beliefs and actions.

6. Affirmations can seem simple, but they are a powerful tool that helps shift one's mindset towards positive thinking, which can help to build confidence and create self-fulfilling prophecies.

7. By incorporating affirmations into your daily routine, you can start your new life. Practice them daily.

Chapter 2: How do you START your new life?

"As a single footstep will not make a path on the earth, so a single thought will not make a pathway in the mind. To make a deep physical path, we walk again and again. To make a deep mental path, we must think over and over the kind of thoughts we wish to dominate our lives."

— Henry David Thoreau

To *start a new life* is both exhilarating and intimidating. Whether you are moving to a new city, starting a new job, or simply trying to turn a new leaf, the process can often feel overwhelming. However, with the right mindset and approach, starting over can be a positive and rewarding experience.

In this chapter, you will learn *20 tips* for starting your new life on the right foot. This chapter aims to provide you with the guidance you need to take steps towards a brighter future. You will learn about setting realistic goals, finding new hobbies and interests, and seeking support from others. Whether you are starting over after a difficult period in your life or simply looking to make a change, these tips will help you take control of your life and move forward with confidence. So, if you are ready to start your new life, read on for some valuable insights and advice. Remember, there are several ways to start your new life.

Here I share with you the *top 20 steps or tips* to do the same.

Let us start!

1. Identify and Prioritize Your Goals

Identifying and prioritizing goals is an important part of living a new life. The first step is to identify what it is you want to achieve. Once you have identified your goals, you can then prioritize them based on their importance and urgency. This allows you to focus on the most important goals first and devote the resources to them.

It is also important to remember that goals should be realistic and achievable. By setting attainable goals, you are more likely to stay motivated and be successful in achieving them. Identify and prioritize your goals, then break them down into smaller, more manageable tasks so that you can track progress and celebrate milestones.

By following these steps, you can set yourself up for success and reach your goals.

2. Create a Vision Board

A vision board is an effective tool to help focus on reaching personal and professional goals. It involves creating a physical or digital board filled with images, quotes, and other motivators to help guide and inspire.

When creating a vision board, it is important to be intentional and mindful of the words and images chosen, as they should reflect what you desire and what it will take to reach those goals.

Placing a vision board in a visible area can help keep the goals top of mind and can provide a sense of motivation and direction. Though it is not necessary to have one, a vision board can be a helpful tool in achieving success.

3. Use Positive Self-Talk

Positive self-talk is the practice of speaking to yourselves in a positive, supportive, and encouraging manner. It is an important life skill, which can help to boost self-esteem, increase motivation, and reduce stress and anxiety.

Positive self-talk can help you stay focused on your goals, combat negative thoughts, and maintain a positive attitude. It can challenge negative beliefs and replace them with more positive and realistic thoughts. It can also remind you of your strengths and successes.

By practicing positive self-talk, you can build self-confidence and resilience, enabling you to be better prepared to tackle the challenges that life throws your way.

Positive self-talk is an important tool in maintaining mental wellbeing. It involves talking to yourselves in a positive and encouraging way, rather than focusing on your weaknesses or putting yourselves down. It can help you stay motivated and keep a positive attitude, even in challenging situations.

Positive self-talk can also help to reduce stress and anxiety, while increasing feelings of self-worth and confidence. When engaging in positive self-talk, it is important to focus on your strengths and successes, rather than dwelling on mistakes or weaknesses. It is also helpful to remind yourselves of your goals and ambitions, and to focus on your potential for growth and development.

With consistent practice, positive self-talk can become a powerful tool for leading a happier and healthier life and starting a new life.

4. Connect with Inspiring People

In today's world, it is important to connect with inspiring people in order to stay motivated and uplifted. Making such connections can help to reinforce positive habits and bring positive energy into your lives. Connecting with inspiring people can help to broaden your perspectives and provide you with new opportunities. Whether it is through online communities or in-person meetups, connecting with inspiring people can help to open your minds to new ideas and inspire you to pursue your goals.

To join a supportive network of like-minded people can also help to keep you motivated and pushing towards your goals. Connecting with inspiring people can certainly be a worthwhile investment of time and energy.

To connect with inspiring people can have a profoundly positive effect on your lives. It can motivate you to reach your goals and push your boundaries, while also inspiring you to be the best versions of yourselves.

Learning from those who have achieved success can help you discover your own strengths and weaknesses and develop your own personal strategies for success.

To connect to inspiring people can also help you understand the importance of collaboration; and how you can use your own unique skills to contribute to a collaborative environment. These connections can ultimately help you lead successful and meaningful lives.

5. Take Action and Stay Consistent

Success in any endeavor requires consistent effort and taking action. To stay consistent, first create a plan and a timeline to achieve your goals. A plan should include milestones to measure progress, and it should be easy to evaluate if you are on track or need to adjust. For taking action, set achievable, manageable goals and stick to them. When you face obstacles, take a step back and reassess. Being consistent and taking action will help you stay motivated, and will allow you to gain skills and experience. With commitment and dedication, you will make progress and reach your desired outcome.

Take action and stay consistent. Being consistent is the key to success in any endeavor. It may be difficult to take the first step, but once you have made the commitment to take action, it is important to stay consistent. This means taking proactive steps to reach your goals and continuing to make progress, no matter how small.

Remember, staying consistent requires discipline and dedication, but it is necessary for success. Consistency also allows for more success in the long run, as your efforts will compound and lead to greater growth. By taking action and staying consistent, you will achieve your goals faster and with greater impact.

6. Find Balance in All Areas of Life

Maintaining balance between all areas of life is essential for attaining success and sustaining overall wellness. It is essential to concentrate on one's work and career while also taking the time to cultivate relationships with family, friends, and romantic partners. It is essential to set aside time for physical activity and self-care.

To achieve this balance, it is important to plan and prioritize. Develop a schedule and daily routine that will allow for a healthy balance of work and play. Set aside time for self-care activities such as exercise and relaxation. By carving out time for both professional and personal activities, individuals can create a balanced lifestyle that is essential for overall success.

7. Be Mindful of Your Thoughts

Mindfulness of your thoughts is integral to cultivating a contented and wholesome life. To acknowledge your thoughts enables you to identify any cognitive patterns that could be harmful to your mental health, while also reminding you to stay optimistic.

Once you become cognizant of your thought patterns, you can then take action. By understanding your thought patterns and reactions, you can develop strategies to help you stay grounded and positive in times of distress. Through mindful contemplation, you can also work to accept and embrace your thoughts without judgement, instead recognizing them as opportunities to learn and grow.

Although it is difficult to stay mindful of your thoughts and feelings, the rewards of doing so can be profound and life changing. In the end, developing a mindful relationship with your thoughts is an invaluable skill that can help you lead more balanced and fulfilling lives.

8. Visualize Your Success

To visualize success is an important part of achieving success! It is important to create positive mental images of yourself as successful and believe in yourself and your goals.

Visualization can help to create a positive mindset and reinforce positive self-talk. Visualizing success can also help to motivate and empower you to take action towards your goals. Visualize the end goal, the journey it will take to get there; and the feeling of success, and use that as motivation to stay focused and take steps towards achieving your goals. Visualizing success is a powerful tool that can help you reach your potential and become the successful person you want to be.

Fostering a clear vision of success can be a highly effective means of accomplishing objectives. This helps to sustain motivation, encouraging you to remain focused on your objectives. It can promote a proactive attitude and allow greater readiness to explore new options. You can use visualization techniques to cultivate a vision of success.

9. Cultivate Gratitude

Cultivating gratitude in life is an essential part of well-being and cultivating a positive outlook.

Taking the time to pause and be mindful of the positive aspects of life can help reduce stress and promote resilience. Practicing gratitude can also help increase feelings of connection to others, as gratitude often leads to an increase in kindness and generosity.

Practicing gratitude can help to create a cycle of positivity, leading to greater well-being. Incorporating activities such as writing thank-you note, reflecting on positive experiences, or keeping a gratitude journal can help to strengthen and reinforce the practice of gratitude. It may be helpful to recognize opportunities to express gratitude daily, such as thanking someone for their help or considering the positive aspects of a challenging situation. Ultimately, taking the time to cultivate gratitude in life can be a powerful tool for cultivating a more positive outlook.

10. Decide with Intention

Deciding with intention is a key step in achieving success. By taking the time to consider the outcomes of a choice; and how it will affect the present and the future, it can help to ensure that the decision will be the right one. By taking a few moments to evaluate the pros and cons of a decision and taking the time to consider the potential results, one can make sure the outcome is well-thought-out and beneficial in the long run.

Taking the time to slow down and think through a decision can help to ensure that it is the best one for the situation. Taking the time to decide with intention and with consideration for the long-term is essential for success.

Deciding with intention is an important step in achieving desired outcomes and maintaining focus. It involves actively considering what is important and desired, and considering all probable outcomes, before proceeding. Intentional decision-making can help to reduce the chances of making hasty decisions that may not be in line with desired outcomes and may even be counter-productive.

To take the time to analyze and evaluate options, and considering how each decision could benefit or hinder progress, can be an effective way to decide with intention. This approach can help to minimize distractions and ensure that decisions are made with an eye towards what is important and will best benefit an organization, team, or individual.

11. Invest in Yourself

Investing in yourself is an important and often overlooked part of achieving success. Whether it is spending time on self-development, taking classes to learn new skills, exploring new hobbies and interests, or simply taking better care of yourself, self-investment is one of the most beneficial steps you can take.

Doing so not only improves your confidence, wellbeing and work life balance but also allows you to tap into new opportunities and gain a competitive edge. Investing in yourself means making sure, you have the resources, knowledge, and support you need to reach your goals and live a successful and fulfilling life.

To invest in one's personal growth is a key factor in guaranteeing a successful future.

Taking the time to develop skills, cultivate relationships, and prioritize self-care will provide a stable base for future accomplishments. Self-investment can involve a wide range of activities, such as attending industry events or furthering one's education.

12. Practice Self-Care

Practicing self-care is essential for a healthy and balanced life. It involves engaging in activities to reduce stress, maintain emotional health and improve physical well-being. This can include taking time for yourself to relax, engaging in physical activities such as yoga or walking, and making sure, you are eating well and getting enough sleep.

It can involve spending time with friends and family, taking time to meditate or practice mindfulness, or simply indulging in activities you enjoy. Self-care is an important part of maintaining mental and physical health and is critical to the maintenance of a successful career.

You should take the time to practice self-care and build a routine to ensure you are taking care of yourselves.

13. Live with Purpose

To live with purpose is essential to leading an engaged and meaningful life. To live with purpose, one must first identify their values and goals that are most important to them. Once identified, it is important to create a plan of action to make these goals a reality. One should break down larger goals into smaller, achievable steps, or set a timeline for when they should accomplish each goal.

Having a support system to help stay motivated and on track is important. Finally, it is necessary to be open to change and flexible in the face of adversity. With a coherent plan and the right tools, anyone can live with purpose and find fulfillment.

14. Celebrate Your Progress

Celebrating progress is an important component of any successful endeavor. It is often easy to become overwhelmed by the magnitude of a goal, but taking the time to recognize and enjoy each step of the journey helps to keep motivation high and morale even higher. Celebrating progress also serves to encourage innovation and creativity, as successes can spur the development of more ambitious plans.

Celebrating progress is a way of saying thank you to the people involved in the work and serves as a reminder that hard work can yield actual results. Therefore, it is an important part of any successful project to take the time to acknowledge the progress made and enjoy the journey.

Celebrating progress is essential for motivation and success. You can do it in small or big ways, such as congratulating yourself for completing a task or taking a moment to reflect on a major milestone. Showing appreciation for the progress, you have made helps to keep your morale high and keep you going when times get tough.

Celebrating progress also signals yourself that you can achieve your goals, and that success is attainable. It can also affect the atmosphere of your workplace, inspiring others to strive for excellence. To recognize progress can be a powerful and effective way to increase motivation and encourage productivity.

15. Let it go

The 'Let it go' principle is an important life skill that can be beneficial in both your personal and professional lives. It encourages you to accept situations that are beyond your control and to move on from those that are causing you undue stress or hardship.

By practicing this principle, you can develop greater resilience, improve your emotional intelligence and become better communicators. This can lead to improved relationships, both personally and professionally. Sometimes, it can even help to facilitate conflict resolution in the workplace, as it encourages you to be open to different perspectives and to negotiate more effectively. Ultimately, the 'Let it go' principle allows you to stay focused on your goals and to find peace and contentment in your daily lives.

16. Embrace Change

Change is an inherent part of life, and one of the most essential tools for growth and development. It is difficult to embrace, but it is often necessary to progress. To make the most of change, it is important to remain open-minded and willing to learn. There is value in considering all potential outcomes and adapting accordingly. To take risks and experimenting with new technologies can lead to great opportunities. Change is a positive thing, and it can be a valuable experience if used correctly.

It is important to remember that a new opportunity may be just around the corner and not to be afraid of the unknown. A willingness to embrace change can lead to improved processes and overall success.

17. Spend Time with Loved Ones

To take the time to connect with loved ones is a powerful investment in your relationships and your overall well-being. You can express your gratitude to those in your lives, share experiences, and create memories that will last a lifetime. To foster strong relationships, it is important to show that you care by listening, understanding, and supporting one another. There is no greater joy than laughing; and connecting with those; you cherish. When you attempt to spend quality time with your loved ones, you can create a firm foundation of support and connection that will last for years to come.

18. Connect with Nature

To connect with the natural world can be essential for optimizing physical, mental, and emotional health. Acknowledging the beauty of nature can be a powerful tool to manage stress and promote feelings of serenity. Spending time in the outdoors can be beneficial for one's overall wellbeing, providing a positive outlook and beneficial opportunities.

Studies have showed that engaging with nature can offer a variety of advantages, such as reduction of stress, improved mood and self-esteem, and heightened creativity and productivity. One way to reap these benefits is to take part in activities that allow for direct contact with the natural environment.

19. Develop hobbies

Having hobbies is an important part of your lives as it can provide you with new skills and experiences help to reduce stress and keep you active. Hobbies can range from something as simple as reading a book to something more involved, like playing a sport. It is important to remember to be realistic when developing hobbies; start with something that is manageable and achievable and then escalate the difficulty as skills and confidence are built up. It is always a good idea to find a group or community that shares the same hobby and learn from their experiences. To take the time to develop a hobby can be extremely rewarding and can open up many opportunities to pursue and enjoy.

20. Practice journal

Maintaining a journal can be a powerful tool to process experiences, gain insight into one's thoughts and feelings, foster creativity, and hone problem-solving skills. It can serve as a safe space to explore and work through difficult emotions, as well as promote self-awareness.

Journaling is an effective means of self-reflection, allowing individuals to explore their thoughts, feelings, and emotions. Through this practice, individuals can become better acquainted with their internal processes and work through any personal matters that may arise. There is a variety of approaches to journaling, such as writing freely, incorporating prompts, or using a specific method.

To sum up, beginning a new life can be scary, but it can also be an enjoyable experience.

By using these 20 tips, you can take charge of your life and build the future you desire.

Remember, it is necessary to set goals, keep a positive attitude, and give yourself time. Change may not happen right away, but if you work hard and stay determined, you can make your dreams come true. So, *take a deep breath, enjoy the ride, and begin living the life that you deserve.*

***

Key Takeaways - 2

1. To *start a new life* is both exhilarating and intimidating.

2. Here, I share with you the *top 20 tips* to start a new life:

I.	Identify and Prioritize Your Goals
II.	Create a Vision Board
III.	Use Positive Self-Talk
IV.	Connect with Inspiring People
V.	Take Action and Stay Consistent
VI.	Find Balance in All Areas of Life
VII.	Be Mindful of Your Thoughts
VIII.	Visualize Your Success
IX.	Cultivate Gratitude
X.	Decide with Intention
XI.	Invest in Yourself
XII.	Practice Self-Care
XIII.	Live with Purpose
XIV.	Celebrate Your Progress
XV.	Let it go
XVI.	Embrace Change
XVII.	Spend Time with Loved Ones
XVIII.	Connect with Nature
XIX.	Develop hobbies
XX.	Practice journal

3. By using these 20 tips, you can take charge of your life and build the future you desire.

4. So, *take a deep breath, enjoy the ride, and begin living the life that you deserve.*

Chapter 3: My START formula

Are you fed up with feeling like you are going nowhere?

Are you longing for an exciting new journey?

Well, my friend, it is time to **START**!

There are several ways to transform life. It is a good thing, is not it? You have just completed reading the top 20 tips in the previous chapter. I will introduce here my *START formula* for transforming your life.

Are you ready?

Charles R Swindoll once said, *"Life is 10% what happens to us and 90% how we respond."*

This popular saying reflects a belief that your experiences in life are not solely the result of external forces, but your reaction to them. You have control over your lives, and your response to any situation can have a significant impact on your future experiences. This suggests that there is a responsibility that comes with your ability to choose your response, and that in order to lead a fulfilling life, you must be mindful of your reactions.

Always keep in mind, this encourages you to take ownership of your experiences and be cognizant of your reactions, as these can have a major influence on your life.

Cognitive-behavioral theory, which states that your thoughts, feelings, and behaviors are all interconnected, and that your perception of a situation can have a significant impact on how you respond to it, supports this idea. For example, if you perceive a life event as a challenge or an opportunity, your response to it will be different.

This quote also suggests that your reactions to life experiences have more influence on your lives than the experiences themselves. By being mindful of how you think and feel about your experiences, and taking action that is aligned with your values and goals, you can shift your outlook and take control of your lives.

Are you ready to take the steps to transform your life?

My *START* formula provides a straightforward approach that enables you to make positive changes and break through any internal or external barriers. With this formula, you will gain the clarity, focus, and energy to bring about the desired life transformation. You will identify the root causes of your dissatisfaction, create a plan to reach your goals, and make your dreams a reality. *Take the first step today towards achieving the life of your dreams!*

The *START* formula is like a compass that will guide you towards a brighter, happier future. It is time to stop overthinking and start taking action.

You deserve to live the life of your dreams, and the START formula is the key that will unlock your potential.

Imagine waking up every morning with a sense of purpose and excitement. Imagine feeling energized by the possibilities that lie ahead, rather than weighed down by the monotony of everyday life. This is the life that the *START formula* can help you achieve.

The *START formula* acts as a powerful tool to help you begin your new life journey with confidence and determination. This acronym **(START)** stands for *Stop Overthinking, Taking care of your health; Action is everything, Reading, and teaching.* By adopting these simple yet effective steps, you can overcome your doubts and fears and start living the life you deserve.

The first step, *Stop Overthinking*, helps you to overcome your doubts and fears, and focus on the present moment. It is easy to get caught up in overthinking and worrying. You often get so caught up in your minds that it's difficult to take action. You felt like your thoughts were spiralling out of control and that you have no control over the situation. It is important to remember that action is key. Taking action is the only way to get out of the cycle of worrying and make progress.

The second step, *taking care of your health,* is crucial for personal growth and success, as it helps you to maintain your physical and mental well-being. Making sure that you are taking care of your health is also essential. Eating healthy, exercising, and getting enough sleep are crucial for managing stress, staying focused, and getting things done.

The third step, *Action is everything*, is a reminder that taking action is key to achieving one's goals. Always remember the power of reading and teaching (The fourth and fifth step). Reading is a great way to stay informed about topics that are important to you and to gain new insights. Getting knowledge through reading and teaching are important part of personal development, helping people to gain knowledge and share their experiences with others. Reading and teaching can be powerful tools for keeping your mind sharp and your thoughts organized.

By following the *START formula*, you can start your new life journey with clarity, purpose, and motivation.

You must accept it. Your minds start to overthink and worry so much that taking action seems impossible. It is like you are stuck in a mental traffic jam with no way out. But here is the secret: action is the ultimate antidote. By taking action, you break free from the cycle of worry and find a path forward.

Of course, taking action is easier said than done. That is why you need to prioritize your health. Eating well, exercising, and getting enough rest are all vital for managing stress, staying focused, and getting things done. Think of it as fuel for your mind and body!

So, *what are you waiting for?* Stop overthinking, take care of your health, read, teach, and take action. The world is waiting for you to shine, and the *START formula* is the spark that will ignite your fire. Let us do this!

Key Takeaways - 3

1. There are several ways to transform life.

2. Cognitive-behavioral theory states that your thoughts, feelings, and behaviors are all interconnected.

3. Your reactions to life experiences have more influence on your lives than the experiences themselves.

4. The *START* formula is like a compass that will guide you towards a brighter, happier future.

5. This acronym **(START)** stands for

S=*Stop Overthinking,*
T=*Taking care of your health;*
A=*Action is the key (everything),*
R=*Reading, and*
T=*Teach what you know.*

Chapter 4: S=Stop over thinking

Overthinking is something that many people experience. It happens when you think about something too much and get stuck. This can make you feel bad and affect your mental, emotional, and physical health. In this chapter, you will become familiar with different aspects of overthinking, including what it does to you, and ways to stop it.

4.1 What is over thinking?

Over thinking is a habit of ruminating on issues or worrying excessively about a situation. It can be a psychological phenomenon, which can lead to a decrease in productivity as it can take up an individual's attention and energy. It can also lead to feelings of stress, anxiety, and even depression.

While it is normal to experience some level of over thinking from time to time, it can become a problem when it interferes with your daily lives.

What are types of over thinking?

There are several types of over thinking that people may experience. As over thinking is a common issue that can cause a variety of mental health issues, from anxiety to depression, it is important to understand its different types in order to address and manage them.

The first type of over thinking is **rumination**, which is repetitively going over thoughts without taking action. This can involve replaying past events, worrying about future events, or endlessly analyzing a decision.

Rumination can be both **positive and negative**, but your focus should be on the negative aspects of the thought and their remedies.

Cognitive Rumination: One type of over thinking is cognitive rumination. This type of over thinking involves repeatedly going over things in your minds, such as a decision you made or a conversation you had. It can lead to feelings of regret and self-doubt, as you focus on all the things that could have gone differently. You may also expect the worst-case scenario for any situation, believing that something bad will inevitably happen.

Emotional Rumination: Another type of over thinking is emotional rumination. This type of over thinking involves dwelling on your emotions, such as feelings of anger, sadness, or guilt.

The second type of over thinking is **catastrophizing**. This is when someone imagines the worst probable outcome in a situation. It is common for people to think of negative possibilities, but those with catastrophizing will take it to the extreme, believing that the worst potential outcome is certain.

The third type of over thinking is **black-and-white thinking.** This is when a person only sees two sides of an issue. For instance, you may think you are always right or the world's biggest failure. It is a thought pattern that makes people think in absolutes.

Who is an over thinker?

You can define an over thinker as someone who spends too much time thinking about a situation, problem, idea, or decision, often to the point of being unable to take any action.

How do you know you are an over thinker?

Being an over thinker can often be difficult to recognize, as it is easy to assume that everyone else around you is thinking the same amount as you are. However, there are some telltale signs that can help you identify if you are an over thinker.

(i) The first sign is that you are constantly analyzing the situation and events that are happening around you. You cannot help but try to make sense of things and figure out the best way to go about solving any situation. Your mind seems in constant overdrive, constantly questioning and looking for answers. You can easily become overwhelmed or frustrated when you do not have all the answers or do not understand something.

(ii) Another common trait of an over thinker is that you are often anxious or stressed in situations that you do not have complete control over. You may be worried that something bad is going to happen if you make the wrong decision or if something does not.

(iii) The sign of being an over thinker is when you spend too much time considering all workable solutions to a problem. You may endlessly go over the same ideas, analyzing all the pros and cons, without ever deciding or taking any action. This can make it difficult to take on new tasks or activities, as the potential outcomes of each decision may overwhelm you.

(iv) Another sign of being an over thinker is when you are stuck in a loop of worrying or rumination. You may go over the same thoughts.

"People become attached to their burdens sometimes more than the burdens are attached to them." — **George Bernard Shaw**

Is Over thinking same as Negative Thinking?

Overthinking, though, is driven by negative self-talk. It differs from negative thinking.

As you now know, *over thinking* is an activity that involves putting too much thought into an issue or problem. This is most easily displayed when a person thinks about something over and over, thinking about probable outcomes and thinking things through, even when the result or outcome does not change.

Whereas *negative thinking* means a pattern of thinking negatively about yourself and your surroundings. It can fog your minds, blocking your ability to think clearly. Negative thoughts can make you feel anxious, sad, or pained. It can touch you mentally and/ or physically.

4.2 Why is over thinking dangerous?

Over thinking can be a dangerous habit for many individuals, leading to increased stress and anxiety levels. Constantly worrying over events and decisions that have already happened or will may happen can drain and detriment your overall wellbeing. It can lead to a cycle of feeling overwhelmed and desperate to find answers or solutions.

As you loop through these thoughts and feelings, your minds become fogged and you cannot see the bigger picture clearly. It can lead to missed opportunities and even to an inability to move forward. By understanding the dangers of over thinking, you can work to improve your mental health and create healthy habits for yourselves.

You will explore here why over thinking is so dangerous and what you can do to reduce its effects. You will also learn tips on how to break the cycle of over thinking.

1. It can lead to stress and anxiety

Over thinking can be dangerous because it can lead to stress and anxiety.

"Stress, anxiety, and depression can contribute to overthinking. Meanwhile, overthinking may be associated with increased stress, anxiety, and depression." — **Stephanie Anderson Whitmer**, *What is Overthinking...*, GoodRxHealth

When you are stuck in a cycle of over thinking, your brains are working overtime and it can become difficult to think clearly and decide. This can lead to feelings of overwhelm and anxiety that can be difficult to break out of. When you ruminate on your thoughts and worries, it can lead to heightened levels of cortisol, the stress hormone, which can have a detrimental effect on your mental and physical health.

2. It can lead to depression

Over thinking can lead to depression when a person's thought patterns become so negative that it is difficult to find any joy or pleasure in life. As the person's thoughts become increasingly pessimistic, they can feel overwhelmed with the weight of their negative thoughts, leading to a lack of motivation and energy. When these feelings persist over time, depression can set in. Over thinking can lead to a person fixating on their problems, making them feel more out of control and helpless. This can worsen their depression, as they feel powerless to make changes and experience relief.

3. It can make 'decision-making' difficult

When it comes to decision-making, over thinking can be extremely dangerous. The more you over think, the more doubts you will have about your decisions. This can lead to a state of paralysis, where you cannot decide at all. It can also make your second-guess your decisions and question yourself. This can lead to a feeling of constant stress and frustration, and can even lead to depression if you do not manage it properly.

4. It can lead to unhealthy behaviours

One risk of over thinking is that it can lead to unhealthy behaviours. When you ruminate on your problems too much, it can lead to you overindulging in unhealthy activities such as drinking too much, smoking, or overeating. It can also lead to a sense of paralysis, where you feel you cannot take any kind of action. This sense of helplessness can cause you to become stuck in a cycle of over thinking and cannot break free.

"When you don't overthink, you become more efficient, more peaceful, and more happy." — **Remez Sasson**, What is Overthinking and How to Overcome it, SuccessConsciousness.

5. It can cause rumination

Over thinking can cause rumination, which is a repeated cycle of thinking the same thoughts over and over. It is a form of unhealthy and unproductive thinking, which can cause a person to become stuck in a negative spiral of thoughts.

Rumination can often lead to feelings of guilt, shame, and helplessness. It can keep you from seeing the bigger picture, making you unable to take action on anything. It can also increase your stress levels and lead to depression and anxiety. You should strive to prevent rumination to safeguard your mental health and well-being.

6. It can cloud your judgement

Over thinking can cloud your judgement and create a feeling of being overwhelmed. This can cause you to become indecisive and unable to decide—or to make decisions that are not in your best interest. You may also become so focused on a problem that you cannot look at it objectively. For example, you might become so caught up in the details of a personal conflict you cannot see the bigger picture.

7. It can prevent you from living in the present

Over thinking can be an all-consuming problem, one that can prevent you from living in the present. People who over think get stuck in the past, ruminating on past events or worrying about what will happen in the future. This can prevent you from truly enjoying the moment and make it difficult for you to stay focused on the task at hand. It can also lead to feelings of guilt, regret, and low self-esteem. It is important to recognize the effects of over thinking, and to put it in check.

8. It can lead to negative thoughts and destructive thinking patterns

Over thinking is dangerous because it can lead to negative thoughts and destructive thinking patterns. When you over think, you focus on all the potential problems and risks associated with a situation, rather than the potential benefits. You might also obsess about hypothetical and possibilities that may never occur. This type of thinking can lead to anxiety and depression, as you become consumed by your own thoughts and the possibilities of what might go wrong. This type of negative thinking can leave you feeling helpless to find solutions to your problems.

In conclusion, over thinking can be a dangerous trap to fall into. It can cause you to become overwhelmed and cause stress, anxiety, and even depression. It can lead to unhealthy coping mechanisms, such as avoidance, procrastination, and rumination. If you struggle with over thinking, it is important to seek help from a professional and to practice mindfulness and self-care. With the proper support and tools, you can learn to control your thoughts and live a healthier, happier life.

4.3 Why do you over think?

It is natural and normal to take time to think, but sometimes, over thinking can become a problem.

"Man is not worried by real problems so much as by his imagined anxieties about real problems." — **Epictetus**

As you know, over thinking can lead to stress, anxiety, and depression and can make tasks more difficult to complete. When you are stuck in a loop of over thinking, it is difficult to break free and move forward.

Nevertheless, why do you over think in the first place?

It may be (a) a symptom of certain psychological disorders, or it might be (b) caused by a variety of external factors or physiological factors.

You will explore here the various causes of over thinking, the consequences that can come from it, and how to overcome it.

1. Fear of making the wrong decision

One of the most common reasons people tend to over think is because they have a fear of making the wrong decision. You can root this fear in feelings of insecurity, a lack of self-confidence, or a fear of failure. People may worry that others will judge them if they make the wrong decision or that they will be stuck with the consequences of their decision. This fear can cause people to become stuck in an endless cycle of rumination and analysis, making it difficult for them to move forward.

2. Difficulty trusting your own judgement

One of the main reasons people over think is because they have difficulty trusting their own judgement. This can also come from a lack of self-confidence, or from a fear of making the wrong decision. When you lack confidence in your ability to decide, it is easy to get caught up in second-guessing everything and trying to analyze every probable outcome before taking action. This can lead to an endless cycle of over thinking, as it becomes harder and harder to decide. To break out of this cycle, it is important to take a step back and focus on building your confidence in your own judgement.

3. Comparing yourself to others

Comparing yourself to others is one of the most common reasons people over think. When you compare yourselves to others, it is difficult to find perspective and fully appreciate your own achievements. You can become wrapped up in thoughts of "what if" and "if only", and worry about how you measure up to your peers.

Comparing yourselves to others can lead to feelings of insecurity and a lack of self-confidence. It is important to remember that everyone has their own unique set of strengths and weaknesses, and that there is no one "right" way to live your life.

4. Over thinking the consequences

Over thinking the consequences of a situation can be a major source of over thinking. This type of thinking often leads to us focusing on the worst-case scenarios and worrying about the future. You can get stuck in a loop of trying to figure out what the consequences of your actions might be, or worrying about all the things that could go wrong. This can be very harmful, as it prevents you from taking action and can paralyze you with fear. It is important to remember that most of the time your over thinking is based on assumptions, and yet you give them more weight than the actual reality of the situation.

5. Fear of failure

One of the most common reasons people over think is fear of failure. You may fear failure because it carries a negative connotation and you are afraid of the disappointment or criticism that might come with it. You may also be afraid of the unknown or uncertain outcomes of a situation, which can lead to over thinking and indecision. Fear of failure can cause you to become so focused on potential outcomes that you cannot take action. Facing your fears and developing a healthy relationship with failure is key to overcoming over thinking.

6. Trying to control the outcome

Over thinking often occurs when you are trying to control the outcome of a situation. You may obsessively focus on the details, and worry about how things could turn out. You may also second guess yourselves and your decisions, or try to expect how other people will respond to your actions. This type of over thinking can leave you feeling helpless and stressed, as you cannot predict the future.

Kahlil Gibran says, *"Our anxiety does not come from thinking about the future, but from wanting to control it."*

The best way to combat this type of over thinking is to focus on the present moment and focus on the things you can control, such as your attitude and your actions. Recognizing that you cannot control the outcome of everything can help reduce the pressure you place on yourself.

7. Perfectionism

Perfectionism is another common cause of over thinking. Perfectionists have incredibly high standards for themselves and focus on their mistakes and shortcomings, rather than on their successes. This can lead to a cycle of rumination and worrying about not measuring up to the standards they have set for themselves. Perfectionism-fueled over thinking can be a major obstacle to achieving goals, as it can lead to procrastination and feelings of overwhelm. It can also lead to undue stress and anxiety, preventing you from enjoying the present moment.

8. Ruminating on the past

Ruminating on the past is a common form of over thinking. When you do this, you are constantly rehashing past events, conversations, and any mistakes you have made. You spend too much time trying to figure out what went wrong and why things happened the way they did. This kind of rumination can be incredibly draining, both mentally and emotionally. It can also lead to intense feelings of guilt, regret, and sadness. If you find yourself caught in a loop of rehashing the past, it is important to remind yourself that dwelling on the past will not help you move forward—in fact, it may make things worse. Instead, try to focus your energy on the present and take action to create a positive future.

In conclusion, over thinking can often result from feeling overwhelmed by a situation. It is difficult to control your thoughts and break out of a pattern of over thinking, but it is possible. Taking breaks, engaging in physical activity, and finding a distraction can help to reduce the urge to over think. Seeking professional help is also an option for those who require more help in dealing with their over thinking. It is important to recognize when you are over thinking and try to challenge the irrational thoughts. Taking a step back to evaluate the situation can help to reduce the time spent over thinking.

4.4 How to stop over thinking?

Over thinking can be a crippling habit, leading to mental exhaustion and lack of clarity. It can cause a person to ask himself or herself questions constantly, second-guess their emotions, and lead to unhealthy behavior. One can also see it as a sign of brilliant intellect and a valuable asset for problem solving. However, how will you stop overthinking?

As Lord Buddha and his followers were travelling, they stopped to rest by a lake. One disciple asked Lord Buddha how to calm a mind that was plagued with disruptive thoughts. Sitting beneath a tree, Lord Buddha replied he was feeling thirsty and requested the disciple to bring him some water from the lake.

Upon arriving at the lake, the disciple noticed it was being used for washing clothes and utensils, so he went further in search of clean, freshwater. Just as he was about to collect the water, a bullock cart passed by and the lake became muddied. After waiting for some time, it became apparent that the water would remain muddied, so the disciple could not fulfil Lord Buddha's request.

The disciple returned to Buddha and informed him of the lake's muddy water. An hour later, Buddha asked the disciple to return to the lake and collect the water. As instructed, the disciple went back and could find freshwater. He filled the jar and brought it back to Buddha.

Lord Buddha looked at it and said, *"Do you see how the water in this jar was once just like the water in the lake? It was murky and unclear. But when you waited patiently, the mud settled and allowed the water to become clear again. Your mind is the same way. When you have disruptive thoughts and emotions, do not force them away. Allow them to settle like the mud in the water, and eventually, your mind will become clear again."*

As Lord Buddha and his followers continued their journey, the disciple looked back at the lake and marveled at how such a simple lesson could have such a profound impact on his life. He felt grateful to have learned from the grand master and vowed to share this lesson with others who were struggling with turbulent thoughts and emotions.

The moral of the story is clear.

Remember, one of the most important aspects of mental health and well-being is your ability to remain balanced between thought and action. Too much thought can lead you to a state of over thinking, where you are constantly analyzing and rehashing your thoughts and decisions to achieve perfection. While this can be productive when used to assess challenging situations and problem solving, it can also be unhealthy when your thoughts become centered on worry and anxiety.

What are the ways to stop overthinking?

Here are five important ways to do it.

1. Identifying when you are over thinking

One of the most important steps to managing over thinking is recognizing when it is happening. When you are over thinking, your thoughts spiral and become more and more intense, and it is hard to break out of that cycle. If you felt overwhelmed, anxious, or stressed, it may be a sign that you are over thinking. Pay attention to your thought patterns and take steps to focus your attention elsewhere if you notice yourself becoming overly focused on one particular issue.

"Rule number one is, don't sweat the small stuff. Rule number two is it's all small stuff." — **Robert Eliot**

2. Changing your thought process

One way to reduce over thinking is to change your thought process. When faced with a difficult or uncomfortable situation, simply stop, observe your thoughts, and reframe them in a more positive way. This involves being mindful of your thoughts and consciously refocusing. For example, if you are feeling anxious about a situation, ask yourself if the worrying is helping you, or if it is only making you feel worse. If the answer is the latter, try to reframe the situation in a more optimistic light. Focus on the things you can control, like your attitude and how you are reacting to the situation.

"Everyone does stupid things they regret. I, for one, do them daily. So stop your downward spiral by heaving a big sigh and saying, 'OK, that happened.' And then move on."—**Ellen Hendriksen,** Toxic Habits: Overthinking, ScientificAmerican

3. Understanding the causes of over thinking

Understanding the causes of over thinking is key to overcoming the habit. Stress, worry, fear, and anxiety can all lead to over thinking. When you are constantly worrying about things or feeling anxious, it is easy to get stuck in a loop of rumination and negative thinking. Other common causes of over thinking include low self-esteem, perfectionism, a need for control, or negative core beliefs.

By being aware of what triggers over thinking, you

can work to identify and address the root causes. For example, if low self-esteem is contributing to over thinking, you can focus on building your self-esteem and gaining more confidence in yourselves.

4. Practicing meditation and mindfulness

One of the most important things you can do to combat over thinking is to practice meditation and mindfulness. This practice teaches you to realize our thoughts, feelings, and physical sensations without judgement. It helps you to understand how your thoughts and feelings are influencing your behavior and how to respond to them in helpful and positive ways. Meditation and mindfulness can also help you recognize your patterns of over thinking, and to become more aware of when and why you are over thinking. This can help you make healthier and more balanced decisions, and to be more mindful of your reactions to situations.

5. Talking to someone about your worries

Talking to someone about your worries can be one of the best things to do if you find yourself over thinking. Talking to a friend, family member, or even a mental health professional can be incredibly beneficial to you. It not only helps to get your worries off your chest, but it also gives you an outside perspective and can help you find clarity. Talking to someone can help to build your self-confidence and strengthen your relationships with those around you.

In conclusion, over thinking can be a huge impediment to your happiness and success. It can cause you to doubt yourselves, feel overwhelmed, and ignore your intuition.

It is important to recognize when you are over thinking, and to stop it. Some strategies to help manage over thinking include practicing mindfulness and meditation, taking a break from the situation, talking to a trusted friend, and getting out of your comfort zone. By taking action, you can prevent over thinking from taking over your lives.

Key Takeaways - 4

1. Over thinking is a habit of ruminating on issues or worrying excessively about a situation.

2. You can define an over thinker as someone who spends too much time thinking about a situation, problem, idea, or decision, often to the point of being unable to take any action.

3. Overthinking, though, is driven by negative self-talk. It differs from negative thinking.

4. Over thinking can be a dangerous habit for many individuals, leading to increased stress and anxiety levels.

5. You do over thinking because:

  * Fear of making the wrong decision;
  * Difficulty trusting your own judgement;
  * Comparing yourself to others;
  * Over thinking the consequences;
  * Fear of failure;
  * Trying to control the outcome;
  * Perfectionism;
  * Ruminating on the past.

6. Here are five important ways to stop overthinking:

1. Identifying when you are over thinking
2. Changing your thought process
3. Understanding the causes of over thinking
4. Practicing meditation and mindfulness
5. Talking to someone about your worries.

Chapter 5: T=Take care of Your Health

In today's fast-paced world, it is easy to become consumed by the demands of daily life. Juggling work and a social life can leave little time for self-care, but the consequences of neglecting one's health can be severe both in the short and long-term. As an intelligent individual, it is crucial for you to prioritize self-care by ensuring physical, mental, and emotional well-being in both personal and professional spheres. This chapter outlines ways to achieve optimal health, including a balanced diet, sufficient sleep, and exercise. Investing in one's health yields benefits such as increased productivity, improved decision-making skills, and an overall better quality of life. Whether you are a busy executive or a new professional, or a student, self-care is essential for success and happiness.

5.1 Importance of Holistic health

The stresses of modern life often prevent you from giving adequate attention to your physical and mental wellbeing. However, it is important to remember that health is not just necessary for survival, but also plays a significant role in determining your overall quality of life. It can affect your ability to perform daily activities, pursue hobbies, and spend time with loved ones. Therefore, it is essential to prioritize your health to achieve a fulfilling life.

Health is not merely an individual matter; it also has broader implications for society. The health of a population can affect a country's economy, politics, and social dynamics. Poor health can lead to reduced productivity, increased healthcare costs, and shorter life expectancies. Conversely, promoting good health can improve the physical, mental, and financial wellbeing of individuals and communities.

To achieve optimal health, you must adopt a holistic approach. Holistic health is a lifestyle that considers various factors, including physical, mental, emotional, and spiritual wellbeing. By prioritizing your health in this way, you can improve your overall wellbeing and contribute to a healthier society.

Here are the top 10 reasons for you to maintain your health:

1. Health is the foundation of a happy life.

Adopting a holistic approach to health is essential for a fulfilling life. Prioritizing holistic health means recognizing that it is not just about being illness-free, but about achieving a balance in all aspects of life. By taking care of your bodies through exercise, nourishing food, adequate rest, and stress management, you can improve not only your physical health but also your mental and emotional wellbeing. This balanced lifestyle forms the foundation for a happy and satisfying life. It is important to remember that maintaining good health is a lifelong journey, but the effort is worth it to enjoy a quality of life that is fulfilling and rewarding.

Taking care of yourselves is an act of self-love that should be a top priority.

2. Taking care of your body is the ultimate form of self-love.

Maintaining holistic health and a positive lifestyle involves taking care of your body, which is often compared to a temple. This may sound like a cliché, but it is the ultimate act of self-love. Your body is unique and deserves to be nurtured in the best way possible.

By adopting a holistic approach to health, you are not only taking care of your physical body through exercise and proper nutrition, but also paying attention to your emotional and mental well-being through practices like meditation. Living a healthy lifestyle involves prioritizing your self-care routines and making choices that align with your well-being.

It is crucial to remember that a healthy lifestyle is not just about being disease free, but also about having vitality, energy, and overall well-being. When you take care of your body, you are creating a foundation for a fulfilling life. You will notice that you have more energy, clearer skin, and a more positive outlook on life. So, always remember to prioritize your health and well-being.

3. Good health is the key to achieving your goals and dreams.

A holistic lifestyle that prioritizes well-being is vital for reaching your aspirations and fulfilling your dreams. When you are healthy in mind, body, and spirit, you unlock the boundless energy and clarity necessary to conquer obstacles and pursue your passions.

Every day, commit to making choices that promote your health, such as nourishing your body with nutritious food, engaging in regular physical activity, getting ample rest, and practicing self-care techniques that promote your mental health. By prioritizing your health, you create a solid foundation of vitality that empowers you to achieve your dreams with ease, focus, and joy.

4. A healthy body allows you to enjoy life to the fullest.

Imagine feeling unstoppable, full of boundless energy and radiating vitality. That is what prioritizing your health can do for you. When you take care of yourself, you are able to face any challenge that comes your way with confidence and resilience. You can dive into your passions and hobbies with vigor, and travel and explore the world with ease. A healthy body unleashes a world of possibilities and opportunities, allowing you to fully embrace all that life offers. So, choose to invest in your health today, and let your vibrant spirit shine through!

5. Your health affects the surrounding people, so take care of yourself for their sake as well.

Your health is your greatest asset, and it is time to prioritize it! Remember that your well-being influences not only your own life but also those around you. You have the power to inspire others by leading a healthy lifestyle, making better food choices, and staying active.

Take care of yourself for the sake of your loved ones and watch as your positive choices ripple through your relationships and strengthen your bond. By nurturing your holistic health, you will not only improve your own life but also create a ripple effect of positivity that will inspire others to live their best lives. So go out there, take care of yourself, and inspire those around you with your commitment to holistic health!

6. Good health gives you the energy you need to tackle challenges and overcome obstacles.

Embrace the power of holistic health and lifestyle practices to unlock your potential and achieve greatness! Your energy is the key to conquering life's obstacles and challenges. When you prioritize your health, you not only achieve physical fitness, but you also gain the mental strength required to overcome any hurdle. Imagine facing multiple challenges, feeling weak and unwell. It is nearly impossible to be productive or achieve anything of substance. However, when you are in good health, you have the energy and focus to tackle each challenge with confidence and determination. Prioritizing your health and well-being empowers you to take on any challenge that life throws at you and emerge victorious! Therefore, take care of yourself by creating a holistic approach to your lifestyle.

7. Your body is your temple, so treat it with respect and care.

Your body is your temple, a precious machine that deserves the utmost respect and care. You have the power to fuel your body with healthy food and exercise, as well as to give it rest and relaxation. Every choice you make affects your long-term health and well-being. By choosing to prioritize your health and making daily choices that support your body, you are setting yourself up for a lifetime of wellness and happiness. So, honor your body and its potential by embracing a healthy lifestyle that will help you feel your best and reach your optimal potential. You can amaze things, and it all starts with taking care of yourself inside and out.

8. A healthy lifestyle can help prevent chronic diseases and prolong your life.

You are the master of your own health destiny! Do not wait until it is too late to prioritize your well-being. By embracing a healthy lifestyle, you will be able to ward off chronic illnesses and extend your time on this beautiful planet. Fuel your body with a well-rounded diet, exercise regularly, and attain optimal health. A diet chock full of essential nutrients and vitamins will give your immune system a much-needed boost, which can lower your risk of heart disease and diabetes. Exercise is not just for the body, it is also for the mind, easing anxiety and reducing stress.

9. A healthy mind and body go hand in hand, so prioritize both.

You need to make sure you are living a healthy lifestyle that includes physical activity, eating well, getting enough sleep, and managing stress. By focusing on both your mental and physical health, you can experience many benefits, like having more energy, feeling better emotionally, thinking more clearly, and having a lower risk of chronic diseases.

It is important to think about being healthy both physically and mentally. To be physically healthy, you need to eat healthy foods, exercise regularly, and get enough sleep. To be mentally healthy, you can do things like meditating, being kind to yourself, and doing things that make you happy. Building good relationships with others and feeling good about yourself are also important for mental health. Remember, your emotional and mental health are just as important as your physical health, and being healthy can make you feel better overall.

Therefore, it is important to prioritize your health in all areas of your life, because investing in your well-being means investing in a healthier and happier future for yourself. To achieve overall wellness, you need to make sure you live a holistic lifestyle since a healthy mind and body are interconnected.

10. Remember that investing in your health now will pay off in the long run.

Investing in your health and leading a healthy lifestyle can improve your quality of life now and in the future. Each decision you make today affects your tomorrow, so it is important to invest in your health to create a happier, more productive life. Choose to prioritize your overall health and make choices that positively impact your body, mind, and spirit. Do not wait until it is too late to take care of yourself. Start building healthy habits now that will help you live a vibrant and joyful life.

In conclusion, your health is a priceless treasure that you possess. It is vital to give utmost importance to your physical, mental, and emotional well-being in order to lead a life filled with joy and contentment.

Embrace a balanced diet, make exercise a part of your routine, ensure sufficient rest, and effectively manage stress. These simple yet powerful practices can remarkably transform your life by warding off ailments, boosting your energy, and elevating your overall quality of life. Remember, a sound body and sound mind are the building blocks of a life that radiates happiness and success.

5.2 Powerful Healthy Habits

To feel good and stay healthy, it is important to develop good habits. Taking care of yourself by following a routine can help you lower stress, sleep better, and stay active. Being active and eating healthy foods is important for your general health.

It is hard to keep up with good habits when life gets busy, but it is important for your overall health. It takes a lot of work to make healthy habits stick, but the benefits are worth it. Good habits can make you feel better physically and mentally and help protect you from sickness.

You will learn here the *top 10* powerful healthy habits that can really make a difference.

1. Drink water.

One of the most simple and efficacious habits that one can adopt is regular hydration through water consumption. Adequate hydration is crucial for the optimal functioning of the human body, and water represents the most cost-effective and calorie-free means of quenching thirst.

The adoption of a routine that includes a consistent supply of water through carrying a receptacle at all times, along with the establishment of reminders to drink water at regular intervals, can yield a remarkable impact on energy levels, skin health, digestion, and overall well-being.

Such effects are rooted in the scientific understanding of the role of water in maintaining homeostasis and the proper functioning of a range of bodily systems. Thus, it is recommended that individuals prioritize the incorporation of regular water consumption into their daily routines to achieve maximum health benefits.

2. Eat fruits and veggies

Recent studies have shown that incorporating fruits and vegetables into one's daily diet can have a significant positive impact on overall health and well-being. These natural sources of essential vitamins, minerals, and fiber offer many benefits, including but not limited to weight management, improved digestion, and reduced risk of chronic diseases. By replacing processed snacks with fresh produce, individuals can satisfy their cravings while simultaneously supporting their body's nutrient requirements. Scientific evidence suggests that consuming fruits and vegetables as a regular part of one's diet can lead to increased longevity and decreased risk of many health complications. As such, it is strongly recommended to include these wholesome options in daily meals and snacks.

3. Take the stairs and prefer to walk

To optimize the physiological benefits of physical

activity, it is recommended to eschew the use of elevators and instead engage in stair climbing. This activity elicits an increase in blood flow, elevates heart rate and engages many muscle groups. It provides a convenient means of engaging in exercise with no specialized equipment or facilities. Climbing stairs engenders a sense of accomplishment and may even inspire one to aspire to compete in stair-climbing competitions. Therefore, you can encourage individuals to approach stair climbing with the same fervor and dedication as Olympians, and to adopt this healthy habit as part of a sustainable lifestyle.

4. Move your body

The cultivation of robust, healthy habits is a vital pursuit for the promotion of physical and emotional wellness. Research has shown that engaging in rhythmic, dance-like movements is one of the most enjoyable and effective means of elevating cardiovascular health and stimulating energy flow throughout the body. Besides the calorie-burning and muscle-toning benefits, dancing triggers the release of endorphins, which has been linked to the reduction of stress and the promotion of positive moods.

It is noteworthy that one does not require professional dance training or access to upscale studios to garner these benefits; simply listening to a preferred playlist and allowing the rhythm to guide one's movements can suffice. Whether it is an individual dance party in the privacy of one's home or a group class in a studio setting, incorporating rhythmic movement into one's routine can prove to be a valuable asset to the holistic wellness of the body, mind, and spirit.

5. Meditate

By engaging in meditation, a habit commonly overlooked, one can expect many benefits, ranging from reduced stress and anxiety, to improve focus and memory. Engaging in this practice, one can attain inner peace and clarity amidst the chaos of life. It has established the efficacy of meditation through empirical research, which underscores its potential to bring about remarkable changes in the mind and body. Even a few minutes of daily practice can help hone this skill, enabling one to reap its powerful effects. You should incorporate meditation into their routine for optimal well-being.

6. Get enough sleep

Sufficient sleep is a fundamental component of human health and wellbeing. Sleeping is not just a routine, but also a critical habit that causes the body's repair and rejuvenation. Sleep is akin to a system reset button that is essential for optimal functioning. To optimize this process, one must approach it as a professional napper. The benefits of adequate sleep are countless, including increased energy, improved cognitive function, strengthened immunity, and enhanced mood. Therefore, one should regard sleep as a crucial priority to transform one's life positively.

7. Surround yourself with positive vibes

Scientific research has showed a direct correlation between the energy you emit and the energy you attract from your surroundings. Surrounding oneself with positive vibes is not a trivial, new-age concept, but a factual phenomenon. Individuals who consistently harbor pessimistic thoughts and

Associate themselves with negative individuals are prone to attracting negative energy. Considering this, it is essential to foster positivity by identifying and eliminating negative influences in one's life. It is imperative to seek individuals and situations that uplift and motivate you to be the best versions of yourselves. It is crucial to remember that you have control over the energy you attract, and therefore, it is essential to choose wisely. Emphasizing positive vibes will inevitably lead to an influx of positivity in your lives.

8. Learn something new every day

In an era characterized by the rapid pace of change and discovery, human beings are driven by an innate desire to gain knowledge. The cultivation of lifelong learning habits is a formidable and healthy undertaking that can have a myriad of positive effects on your lives. It promotes curiosity, sharpens cognitive abilities, and unlocks many opportunities. The pleasures of discovering novel concepts and ideas daily are immeasurable. To gain fresh knowledge, one can read, listen to podcasts, experiment with new recipes, or change one's daily commute without enrolling in a formal educational program. Cultivating a curious mindset and being receptive to novel experiences is key. You should not regard to age and experience as impediments, rather, see them as opportunities to expand your horizons and embrace the limitless possibilities of daily learning.

9. Practice gratitude

The empirical evidence is clear: the practice of gratitude is a potent elixir for enduring happiness.

Through the deliberate cultivation of a thankful mindset, individuals shift their cognitive orientation towards positivity, inducing a cascade of effects that open the door to a world of abundance.

But what precisely does it mean to engage in the practice of gratitude? Far from a mere verbal expression of thanks, gratitude requires a deep-seated appreciation for the myriad blessings that populate one's life, from the profound - such as robust health and loving relationships - to the seemingly trivial - such as a well-brewed cup of coffee or a picturesque sunset.

Accumulating research has showed a panoply of benefits that accrue to those who regularly engage in gratitude practice, including enhanced sleep quality, improved mental health, stronger social ties, and greater resilience in the face of adversity. To reap these rewards, one might begin each day by enumerating several things for which they are grateful.

10. Smile often

The roster of efficacious healthy practices encompasses a plethora of beneficial habits. Among these, the act of smiling frequently, despite its triviality, holds remarkable potential. Smiling cannot only enhance one's own physical and mental well-being, but also to positively influence the individuals in one's immediate environment. You can liken the act of smiling to possessing a superpower that can disseminate joy, positivity, and warmth through a mere muscular contraction of the lips.

Smiling can endow the individual with an augmented

sense of self-assurance, a reduction in stress levels, and an improvement in immune system function. Hence, it is imperative to instill the habit of smiling often, be it in response to humorous stimuli, a tender embrace from a loved one, or simply for the sake of it. The power of a smile is a seemingly negligible gesture that can have a significant impact on your lives and the lives of others.

To culminate, fostering and preserving salubrious inclinations can prove helpful in attaining a contented and satisfying existence. Through the regular enactment of practices such as physical activity, consumption of wholesome sustenance, adequate slumber, meditation, and hydration, you can improve your physical and psychological well-being.

Beginning with modest initiatives and progressively amplifying the intensity and duration of these wholesome routines is crucial in preventing exhaustion and feelings of being burdened. Through resolute commitment, these potent healthful practices may become ingrained and positively influence all facets of your lives.

5.3 Must Do smart ways of holistic health

Recently, the concept of holistic health has gained immense traction as a highly sought-after approach to achieving optimal wellness. This health paradigm emphasizes the crucial interconnectedness between the mind, body, and spirit, advocating for individuals to take a proactive stance in promoting their health via healthy lifestyle habits. Considering the increasing prevalence of chronic ailments and mental health concerns, a pressing need for a comprehensive approach to health has emerged, one that encompasses all aspects of an individual's well-being.

You will learn here imperative smart ways of adopting a holistic approach towards health that can be incorporated into your daily routines. The goal of this topic is to empower you with practical tips and strategies to enhance your well-being, ultimately cultivating a balanced, healthy lifestyle that supports physical and mental health.

1. Engage in regular physical activity

Achieving optimal health is within your grasp! Regular physical activity is the key to unlocking your body's full potential. With just 150 minutes of moderate-intensity exercise per week, you can experience incredible benefits that extend far beyond weight management. Physical activity has been shown to decrease your risk of chronic diseases, including heart disease, stroke, type 2 diabetes, and cancer. The true power of exercise lies in its ability to improve insulin sensitivity, reduce inflammation, and lower oxidative stress. Imagine the possibilities when you prioritize your holistic health through regular physical activity. It is time to make a change for the better—you can do it!

2. Eat a balanced diet

Nourishing your body with a wholesome and balanced diet is the first step towards a vibrant and fulfilling life. By filling your plate with whole grains, fresh fruits, leafy greens, and lean proteins, you are providing your body with the essential nutrients it needs to thrive.

These nourishing foods not only support your physical health but also promote mental clarity, emotional balance, and spiritual harmony. With every bite, you are fueling your body with the goodness it deserves and taking a powerful step towards a life of vitality and purpose. So allow yourself to choose wisely, to savor each flavor, and to embrace the joy of nourishing yourselves from the inside out.

3. Get enough sleep

Getting adequate sleep is a fundamental component of maintaining optimal health and well-being. Not only is sleep vital for the proper functioning of the brain and cognitive processes, but it also plays a critical role in the body's rest and recovery. During sleep, the body engages in essential processes such as protein synthesis and cellular repair, which are critical to the growth and maintenance of tissues and organs. Research suggests that inadequate sleep can lead to an array of health problems, including obesity, diabetes, cardiovascular disease, and impaired immune function. It is thus imperative to prioritize sleep and strive for at least 7-8 hours of high-quality sleep per night to promote optimal physical and mental health.

4. Practice stress-reducing techniques

The power of your mind and body is immense, and your well-being is a direct reflection of how you manage stress. While stress can certainly take a toll on your mental and physical health, you can counteract its negative effects through mindful practices. By engaging in activities like meditation and yoga, you can tap into the calm within you and cultivate inner peace.

These practices not only help you reduce stress levels but also improve your overall health by strengthening your immune systems, promoting better sleep quality and reducing your risk of chronic diseases. You hold the key to your own health and happiness, and by choosing to prioritize self-care and stress-reducing techniques, you can unlock your full potential and live your best lives. So take a pledge to take care of yourselves, both physically and mentally, and make the conscious choice to incorporate practices that nourish your mind and body every day.

5. Limit alcohol consumption

It is imperative that you make conscious choices to maintain your holistic health, including limiting your alcohol intake. By doing so, you are taking a smart and empowering step towards a healthier future. Excessive drinking can lead to severe consequences, such as liver damage, cancer, and mental health issues. As a hepatotoxic substance, alcohol has the potential to cause inflammation and harm to liver cells, which can cause cirrhosis, fibrosis, and even liver cancer.

Studies have linked alcohol consumption to an increased risk of developing certain types of cancer, including breast and colorectal cancer. But fear not. By practicing moderation and limiting your alcohol consumption, you are taking control of your health and minimizing the likelihood of alcohol-related health complications. Make the choice to prioritize your well-being and strive towards a healthier, happier future.

6. Quit smoking

Smoking cigarettes can make you sick. It can cause problems with your heart, lungs, and breathing. When you breathe in cigarette smoke, you take in bad chemicals like nicotine, tar, and carbon monoxide. Nicotine is addictive and can make your heart beat too fast and raise your blood pressure, which can make your heartsick. Tar is a sticky substance that can get into your lungs and make it hard to breathe. Breathing in cigarette smoke takes away the oxygen that your blood needs and makes it hard for your heart to work right. If you stop smoking, you can lower your chances of getting these health problems.

7. Practice good hygiene

Maintaining good overall health requires taking measures to prevent the spread of infectious diseases, and proper hygiene is one of the key practices. This involves regularly washing your hands with soap and water for at least 20 seconds, particularly after using the restroom, blowing your nose, coughing or sneezing, and before eating or handling food. To avoid spreading germs to others or objects, it is important to use covers when coughing or sneezing.

It is also essential to know that infectious diseases can easily spread by touching contaminated surfaces and then touching your nose, mouth, or eyes. Practicing good hygiene habits consistently not only benefits your personal health but also promotes a safer environment for everyone.

8. Schedule regular preventive check-ups

In order to maintain overall health, it is important to

meet regularly with a healthcare professional for check-ups and screenings. These measures can detect potential health problems early on and prevent them from becoming more serious. The frequency of these appointments will vary based on factors such as age, medical history, and current health status.

Healthcare professionals recommend annual check-ups and screenings to keep track of one's health. These appointments may involve lab tests, physical exams, and assessments to determine overall health and identify any potential risks. By scheduling regular appointments and managing your health, you can increase the chances of early detection and potentially avoid complications in the future that could negatively impact your health.

9. Stay social and engage

Being social and interacting with others is important for your overall health. Many studies show that having friends and being part of groups can make you feel better physically and mentally. When you spend time with other people, it can help you feel less lonely, sad, and stressed. It can also make your brains work better, improve your mood, and strengthen your bodies. So, it's a good idea to be social and go to events or clubs with other people to stay healthy and happy.

To sum up, achieving holistic health is a journey of nurturing your body, mind, and soul. With the wise methods shared above, you can elevate your wellbeing and experience a life of abundance. Simple adjustments to your daily routine, such as practicing mindfulness, engaging in physical activities, and getting adequate rest, can cause remarkable transformations in your physical, mental, and emotional health.

Remember, holistic health is a lifelong pursuit, and by dedicating yourself to self-care and making mindful decisions, you can live a more gratifying and harmonious existence. Your path to holistic health begins today!

Key Takeaways - 5

1. Holistic health is a lifestyle that considers various factors, including physical, mental, emotional, and spiritual wellbeing.

2. Here are the top 10 reasons for you to maintain your health:

2.1. Health is the foundation of a happy life.
2.2. Taking care of your body is the ultimate form of self-love.
2.3. Good health is the key to achieving your goals and dreams.
2.4. A healthy body allows you to enjoy life to the fullest.
2.5. Your health affects the surrounding people, so take care of yourself for their sake as well.
2.6. Good health gives you the energy you need to tackle challenges and overcome obstacles.
2.7. Your body is your temple, so treat it with respect and care.
2.8. A healthy lifestyle can help prevent chronic diseases and prolong your life.
2.9. A healthy mind and body go hand in hand, so prioritize both.
2.10. Remember that investing in your health now will pay off in the long run.

3. Good habits can make you feel better physically and mentally and help protect you from sickness.

4. Your path to holistic health begins today!

Chapter 6: A=Action is the Key

Whether it is a dead-end job or uneventful personal life, it is easy to feel lost and unsure of what steps to take towards a more fulfilling life. The key to breaking free from this cycle and creating a new beginning lies in taking action and implementing changes.

In this chapter, you will explore the importance of taking action and implementing changes in order to create a new life. You will look at practical tips and strategies for overcoming common roadblocks and making meaningful progress towards your goals. From developing new habits to seeking new opportunities, you will know a range of actionable steps that you can take to create a fresh start.

6.1 Action is the key to start your new life

Taking action is a key factor in achieving success and starting your new life. In any field, from business to personal development, setting goals and actively working to achieve them is essential. It is easy to become complacent and accept the status quo, but in order to grow and move towards success, action is required. It is not enough to set a goal simply, it is necessary to plan a plan of action and start working to make it happen. No matter how daunting the task, taking the first action step is a crucial component of the journey. So, if you are ready to take that first step towards success, let us begin!

1. Taking action is the only way to make progress

Taking action is the only way to make progress towards a goal. No matter how well you plan, if you do not put your plans into action, nothing will happen. Action requires self-discipline, focus and dedication to stick to your goals and make progress. The key to success is to identify the tasks that need to be done, and then make a plan to do them. When you take action, your efforts will be rewarded with tangible results, helping to boost your motivation and confidence. Taking action is an essential step in turning your dreams into reality. You will surprise yourself with the progress you can make by taking small, manageable steps each day.

2. Focusing on the steps, not the destination

To achieve your goals, it is important to remember that action is key. One way to stay focused and motivated is to focus on the steps, not the destination. It is easy to get bogged down by the result and forget to appreciate the journey. Focusing on the steps that lead to the destination helps keep you from feeling overwhelmed and lost. Breaking tasks down into smaller, achievable goals can make achieving that result more manageable. It is also important to celebrate every milestone along the way, as this will help to keep you motivated and on track.

3. Taking action will make you accountable

Taking action is a key part of any successful journey. When we take action, it held you accountable for your choices, your decisions, and your results. Taking action is not only a way to take ownership of your goals and dreams but also a way to make sure that you are actively pursuing the achievements that you desire. When you take action, you become your own biggest cheerleader, pushing yourselves to do more and be better.

4. Action will lead to success

Taking action is the key to success. Whether it is taking action to start a business, achieve a goal, or change your life. Too often, you get stuck in the planning stages and make no progress. When you take action, you put yourselves in a position to reap the rewards. Taking action gives you the opportunity to learn and grow, make mistakes, and eventually find success. Action leads to success because it gives you the opportunity to take control and create something from nothing. Taking action is the difference between just dreaming of success and actually experiencing it.

5. Taking action will create confidence

Taking action is also a key to creating confidence. When you take action, you have evidence that you can do the thing you set out to do. No matter the size or scope of the task, the act of doing it and succeeding is proof that you can achieve what you set out to achieve. As you take action, you will build your confidence in your ability to take on more challenging tasks, and as you become more confident, you will take on bigger and bigger tasks. Taking action is the only way to build the confidence you need to succeed.

6. Taking action will help you stay motivated

Taking action is an essential key to staying motivated. You may have goals and dreams that you want to achieve, but without taking action, those goals will remain just that—dreams. Taking action is the best way to make sure that you stay motivated to achieve your goals.

Taking action also helps to break down larger goals into smaller, more manageable tasks. This allows you to focus on one small task at a time, which can help build momentum and keep you motivated. Taking action gives you the opportunity to track your progress and adjust your strategy if necessary. Taking action is the only way to make sure that you stay motivated and on track.

7. Taking action will help you achieve your goals

Achieving goals does not just happen; it takes planning and action. Taking action is the key to making progress and achieving your goals. Without action, nothing will happen and you will remain in the same place.

Taking action means you are willing to take the steps to make your dreams a reality. It means you are actively moving closer to your goals. Taking action is essential to make sure you are on track and making progress towards your goals. Taking action requires commitment and dedication, but it will be worth it when you finally achieve your goals.

8. Taking action will help you learn from your mistakes

Taking action is an essential part of learning from mistakes. It helps you to identify what went wrong and understand how to do things differently. It also helps you to develop resilience and overcome obstacles, as you can use your mistakes to learn and do things better.

When you take action, you also gain confidence in your abilities, which can lead to more success in the future. Taking action will allow you to reflect on what went wrong and make plans to improve your processes and habits. Action is a key to success, and it starts with learning from your mistakes.

In short, action is essential to achieving any goal, big or small. It is important to remember that when you take action, you are taking control of your life and taking the steps necessary to make progress. Do not let fear, self-doubt, or procrastination hold you back. Make a plan, get organized, and start taking action today. With a bit of guidance and persistence, you, too, can unlock your potential and make great strides toward your dreams.

6.2 Obstacles in taking actions

Starting a new life is not an effortless task. It means leaving behind what you know and going into something new. This can be hard if you do not know what to do or how to do. It is easy to feel overwhelmed and think bad thoughts about yourself. Others might judge you, too. These things can make it tough to start a new life. But you can do it!

By learning things and having a sympathetic attitude, you can improve your life. You just have to take the first step!

Several common obstacles stop you from taking action to start a New Life. Here are the top five reasons, which are crucial to deal with before you take further action.

A. Fear of the Unknown

Fear of the unknown can create significant obstacles for taking action towards changes in life. When you face the prospect of change, you may become overwhelmed with feelings of uncertainty and anxiety. This fear can prevent you from deciding or taking risks that could ultimately lead to personal growth and development. The unknown can be a daunting prospect, and it is common for you to feel paralyzed by the potential consequences of your actions. However, it is important to recognize that change is a necessary part of personal growth and that taking action towards the unknown can lead to glorious rewards. By acknowledging and confronting this fear, you can change your lives and move towards a brighter future.

B. Lack of Knowledge and Resources

If the path to self-improvement were a highway, a lack of knowledge and resources would be like a major roadblock. The absence of valuable information and essential tools can make it nearly impossible to navigate towards your desired destination. The result? Frustration, disappointment, and even hopelessness. Sometimes, it feels just easier to give up on your dreams altogether.

This is true with areas like career growth, personal development, and education. Without the proper resources, you can find yourselves stranded and unable to move forward. To avoid being stuck in the mud, you must prioritize access to the resources and knowledge you need to reach your full potential and create the lives you truly want.

C. Negative Self-Talk and Doubts

Negative self-talk and doubts can create significant obstacles for you if you are seeking to change your lives. When you allow any negative thoughts to take hold, you create limiting beliefs that can hold you back from taking the steps towards personal growth and development. Doubts about your abilities and self-worth can lead to feelings of insecurity and anxiety, making it difficult to take risks and pursue your goals. Negative self-talk can also lead to a lack of motivation and a sense of defeatism, perpetuating a cycle of inaction and frustration. To overcome these obstacles, it is essential to recognize and challenge negative self-talk and doubts, replacing them with positive affirmations and a growth mindset.

D. Social Pressure and Judgement

Social pressure and judgement can be significant obstacles for changing one's life. Often, you may feel constrained by the expectations of others, whether it is your family, peers, or society. The fear of being judged or ostracized can create a sense of apprehension, leading to inaction and a reluctance to deviate from the norm. This can be challenging when trying to make life-changing decisions or pursue a path that is not widely accepted.

It is important to recognize the impact of social pressure and judgement and develop strategies to overcome these obstacles, such as seeking support from like-minded individuals or focusing on personal values and goals.

E. Financial Difficulties

Financial difficulties can also hinder your ability to take action towards changes in your life. The burden of financial stress can lead to feelings of anxiety, frustration, and hopelessness. It is difficult to focus on changing one's life when the pressing need to meet basic financial obligations takes precedence. The lack of resources and options can hinder your ability to take necessary steps towards achieving your goals. In this way, financial difficulties create a significant obstacle to personal growth and development. Addressing financial challenges through financial planning and education can help you overcome these obstacles and achieve your desired outcomes.

6.3 8 Ways to overcome procrastination

Putting things off until later can really hurt how much you are done, both at work and in your personal life. It can make you feel stressed and stop you from making progress. It might even make you feel bad about yourself. In the end, procrastinating can really make it hard for you to achieve your goals. However, you do not have to give in to procrastination. There are ways to get past it if you try. You will learn here some tips and tricks that can help you beat procrastination and get things done.

By using these techniques, you will be able to stay focused, be productive, and make genuine progress in your work and your personal life.

1. Identify the Reasons for Procrastination

When you put off doing things, it is called procrastination. To stop procrastinating, you need to figure out why you do it. There are lots of reasons, like being afraid of failing, not feeling motivated, not knowing what's most important, not being good at managing time, trying to be perfect, or not thinking much of yourself. Once you know why you procrastinate, you can do things to fix the problem and be in charge of your own actions.

2. Set Realistic Goals

When you want to get things done, it is important to set goals. But if you make goals that are impossible to reach, it can stop you from getting started at all. To avoid this, make goals you can actually achieve. This means breaking down your big goals into smaller steps that are easier to do. You should also give yourself enough time to finish each step, and celebrate when you do! By setting realistic goals, you can make sure you are working towards something you can actually accomplish.

3. Change Your Thoughts

If you have trouble getting things done on time, one way to fix it is by changing how you think. Sometimes, you do not want to start a task because you are too worried about finishing it perfectly. But if you focus on small successes along the way, it can help you feel more motivated to keep going.

It is like climbing a gigantic mountain - if you only look at the top, it can feel too hard. But if you take it step by step, it becomes more doable. You can make a plan with smaller steps and celebrate every time you finish one. This will help you feel encouraged and more likely to finish the whole task.

4. Break Tasks into Smaller Steps

If you have a colossal task to do and you feel you cannot start, try breaking the task into smaller steps. This will make it easier to do because you will not feel so overwhelmed. You can make a plan by thinking about what steps you need to take to complete the task. Then, focus on doing each step one by one. This will help you feel more motivated and proud of yourself for completing each step.

5. Establish Consequences

When you put off doing things, it is hard to get them done. That is why having a punishment or reward for finishing tasks can be helpful. A suitable reward could do something fun or get a special treat. But if you don't finish a task, you might have to give up something you really like. Whatever consequence you choose, it has to be important and something you can actually do. This will help you stay focused and make sure you get things done.

6. Track Your Progress

Keeping track of how you are doing is important if you want to stop procrastinating and reach your goals. When you keep track of your progress, you can look back at what you did well and what didn't work so you can make changes and stay on track.

You can make your own system to track your progress, like using a spreadsheet to write what you did each day, or making a calendar to mark off goals as you finish them.

You can even use a to-do list to make sure you're doing the right things each day. When you know what you need to do and when, it is easier to stay excited and focused on your goal.

7. Reward Yourself

When you finish a task or make progress towards a goal, give yourself a little treat. This will help you stay excited and stick with your plan. It can be something small, like a piece of candy or a cup of tea you like. Alternatively, it can be something bigger, like going to a spa or hanging out with friends. Just make sure it is something that makes you feel good and reminds you of how well you are doing.

8. Ask for Help When Needed

To procrastinate is common, but having someone to help can give you the push you need to finish. If you are feeling stressed about a project, ask someone for support. It could be a friend, family member, coworker, or even an expert. Talking to someone can help you feel better and see the task differently. They can give you advice and help you stay on track.

Remember to be nice to yourself and focus on what you are doing right now. Take small steps to stop procrastinating. Be kind to yourself with positive thoughts and celebrate when you finish a job. These ideas will help you beat procrastination and reach your goals.

Key Takeaways - 6

1. Taking action is a key factor in achieving success and starting your new life.

2. Common Obstacles in Taking Action to Start a New Life are:

A. Fear of the Unknown
B. Lack of Knowledge and Resources
C. Negative Self-Talk and Doubts
D. Social Pressure and Judgement
E. Financial Difficulties

3. Here are the eight tips and tricks that can help you beat procrastination and get things done.

3.1. Identify the Reasons for Procrastination
3.2. Set Realistic Goals
3.3. Change Your Thoughts
3.4. Break Tasks into Smaller Steps
3.5. Establish Consequences
3.6. Track Your Progress
3.7. Reward Yourself
3.8. Ask for Help When Needed

4. Remember to be nice to yourself and focus on what you are doing right now. Take small steps to stop procrastinating.

Chapter 7: R=Read

Reading is an amazing activity that can change your life for the better. It is not just a hobby, it is a way to learn and grow. Whether you read self-help books or stories, it can teach you new things and give you fresh ideas.

This chapter attempts to explain why reading is so important and how it can help you be your best selves. You will learn about the benefits of reading books, and how will you read 100 books in a year.

Are you ready to read more and find new ways to learn and grow through books?

There is so much you can discover and enjoy!

7.1 Why do you read?

Many people love to read books because they are fun and interesting. But did you know books can also help you learn and grow? When you read books, you can get smarter and better at solving problems. You can also learn more about the world and become better at talking with others. Reading can even help you be more creative and confident. It can give you ideas for how to make your community a better place.

So reading books is not just fun, it's also great for you!

The top eight reasons for reading books are:

1. It improves concentration and focus

Reading books is a helpful thing to do because it can make you better at focusing and paying attention. When you read, your brains have to work hard to understand what you are reading and remember it. This helps you get better at concentrating and staying focused. If you practice reading regularly, you can get even better at paying attention to things you need to do. Reading books can help you brood over things and make it easier to understand hard ideas and conversations.

2. It increases knowledge and vocabulary

Reading books can be superb for you! It helps you learn new things and understand the world better. When you read, you can learn about history, science, literature, and more. Reading books can help you learn unfamiliar words and improve your reading skills. This can make you better at talking and writing too! So reading books is a great way to learn and grow.

3. It enhances creativity and imagination

Reading books is a transformative experience that transcends beyond mere improvement of one's reading skills. It unlocks the door to creativity and imagination, empowering you to view the world through the eyes of the characters in the book. By immersing yourself in the words of different authors, you gain a wealth of knowledge and ideas that enrich your mind, nurturing your creative side. As you recognize patterns and themes in different stories and characters, you are inspired to develop your own ideas and stories that can impact the world meaningfully. So, let your mind wander and dive into the pages of a book, for it holds the key to unlocking your boundless potential.

4. It develops analytical skills

Embrace the power of books and unlock the potential within you. Beyond the joy of exploring new worlds, reading is an invaluable tool for developing your analytical skills. By interpreting the information presented, you will learn to connect the dots and uncover hidden insights. With every turn of the page, you will sharpen your problem-solving and critical thinking abilities, while also expanding your vocabulary. In addition, as you grow stronger in your analytical prowess, you will make informed decisions that positively impact all areas of your life. So, let the pages of a book be your guide as you unlock your true potential and unleash your greatness upon the world.

5. It improves communication skills

Immersing oneself in the world of books is a powerful tool to enhance one's communication abilities. Not only does it provide a platform to refine language skills, but it also cultivates a profound sense of critical thinking, deepens comprehension of diverse concepts and renders an unmatched level of eloquence. With each book, you can unlock a new level of self-expression and articulate their thoughts and ideas with grace and precision. Reading not only expands your vocabulary but also sharpens your ability to comprehend and convey messages with ease. Embrace the magic of literature and witness the transformation of a novice communicator to an awe-inspiring orator.

6. It helps to build strong relationships.

Reading gives an opportunity to build strong relationships. The act of reading has the power to shift your perspective and ignite your empathy, allowing you to connect with others in a way that strengthens your relationships. With each word, you expand your understanding of the world, gaining insight into other people's experiences and beliefs. By fully immersing yourself in a story, you can unlock a greater sense of compassion and sensitivity towards those around you. Let the pages of a book inspire you to cultivate meaningful and enduring relationships built on a foundation of understanding and empathy.

7. It creates a sense of empathy

There is no better way to cultivate empathy between yourselves and those around you than through the power of reading. By immersing yourselves in the lives of distinctive characters and their perspectives, you can truly comprehend the intricacies of their experiences. This deep understanding helps you to connect with the emotions and motivations of others, and expands our capacity for empathy. By walking in the shoes of another, you can forge meaningful relationships and gain a profound appreciation for the world. Reading books that explore different cultures, values, and beliefs opens your hearts and minds to the unique experiences of others. You must embrace the transformative power of reading and ignite your souls with empathy and understanding.

8. It boosts self-confidence and self-esteem

When you immerse yourself in a book, you open yourself up to endless possibilities and activate your imagination. With every page you turn, you will discover new perspectives and ideas that will inspire you to dream big and believe in yourself. Through the characters and their experiences, you will gain a deeper understanding of the world and yourself, helping you to grow as a person and become more self-assured. So, pick up a book and let it guide you on a path of self-reflection, discovery, and empowerment. The power to build your confidence is within your reach—all you need to do is turn the page.

In a world that is constantly changing, it is easy to forget the simple things that you can do to improve your life. One of those things is reading books. The act of reading not only expands your knowledge and vocabulary, but it also exercises your minds and develops your empathy.

With every book that you read, you gain insight into the world and the people who inhabit it. You learn about history, culture, and how events are connected. You gain a deeper understanding of yourselves and the human experience.

So, make reading a priority in your lives. Take the time to feed your minds and nourish your souls. Embrace the power of books and the transformative effect that they can have on your lives. For in the pages of a book, you can find inspiration, understanding, and a world of endless possibilities.

7.2 How to read 100 books in a year?

If you are seeking to take on a challenge that will not only improve your reading skills but also expand your knowledge, reading 100 books in a year may be just the task for you.

Are you kidding? No.

It may seem difficult at first, but with the right mindset and resources, anyone can achieve this feat and reap the benefits. Reading books can provide immense joy, insights, and help you achieve success in your personal and professional endeavors. You will learn now the practical steps on how to read 100 books in a year, including identifying suitable books, creating a personalized schedule, and other tips to make the challenge more manageable. So embark on this journey to enriching your minds and expanding your horizons.

1. Make a list of books that you want to read

One of the most crucial steps in achieving the goal of reading 100 books in a year is to create a comprehensive list of books you intend to read. Your list will serve as a guide to help you prioritize and focus on the books you should read first and those that can be postponed. It is also important to diversify your list by including books from different genres and topics to avoid monotony. You could consider adding books on history, science, fiction, biographies, and much more. As you progress, remember to keep track of the books you've read, and continually update your list with new ones.

This way, you will always have something to look forward to and stay motivated.

2. Break down your goal into smaller, achievable goals

When you want to achieve a big goal, it is helpful to break it down into smaller goals that you can actually reach. If you want to read 100 books in one year, you can set a goal to read eight books each month. Then, you can break that goal down even further into weekly goals by aiming to read 2 books per week. This way, you will not feel like the task is too hard, and it will be easier to stay motivated and on track.

3. Set aside a specific time for reading

Reading 100 books in a year is a significant accomplishment that requires dedication and commitment. To reach this goal, it is essential to establish a consistent reading routine. This means setting aside a specific time each day to read, whether it is in the morning, during breaks, or before bedtime. Having a dedicated reading time allows you to focus and make steady progress towards your goal. By conditioning yourself to read regularly, you can build the habit and make it easier to stay on track. Remember, investing time in reading not only expands your knowledge, but also enhances your cognitive abilities and improves your overall well-being.

4. Set reminders for yourself to review what you have read

In reading, it is not just about completing a certain number of books in a year. It's about truly immersing yourself in the material and gaining a deep understanding of the ideas presented. One way to ensure that you are getting the most out of your reading experience is by setting reminders to review what you have read.

Do not just read for the sake of reading - read with intention and purpose. Take the time to reflect on the facts, ideas, and key themes in each book. This review process will not only help you remember and understand the material better, but it will also allow you to identify the main points and key details you can carry with you long after you've finished the book.

Remember, success is not just about the result - it is about the journey and the effort you put in along the way. So, take the time to set reminders, whether it is through a calendar, to-do list, or task management app. Make the commitment to read 100 books in this year.

5. Join a book club

Joining a book club can be an excellent strategy for you if you are seeking to stay motivated and complete your goal of reading 100 books in a year. The sense of accountability, support, and encouragement that comes with being part of a group can provide the push to continue even when things get overwhelming. Connecting with individuals who share a passion for reading can lead to valuable discussions and insights while expanding one's literary horizons. Where physical book clubs may not be available, online book clubs can offer a viable alternative.

Fortunately, there are many virtual book clubs

available that cater to different interests and reading preferences. So, join one.

6. Listen to audiobooks

Unlock the power of audiobooks that will enhance your life in ways you never thought possible. With audiobooks, you can easily absorb knowledge and entertainment while on-the-go, whether you're commuting, working out, or cleaning. The beauty of audiobooks lies in their ability to boost your concentration and comprehension, enabling you to devour more books in a year than ever before. So, let your mind wander and your imagination soar with the help of audiobooks. And don't forget to ramp up the pace with the speed feature, so you can achieve even more. Remember, the possibilities are endless when you open your ears to the wonders of audiobooks.

7. Take notes while reading

As you absorb the knowledge and wisdom within, capture the essence of each chapter by jotting down key points, insightful quotes, and memorable takeaways. These notes will become your treasure trove of knowledge, allowing for easy reference to them and recall the valuable insights you gained. With these notes, you will be able to create a powerful summary of the book, cementing the key concepts in your mind and inspiring others with your newfound wisdom. So, embrace the power of note taking and unlock the true value of each book you read!

8. Track your progress to stay motivated

One of the most vital keys to success is to monitor your progress. It is vital to remain driven and focused, and keeping track of how far you have come is essential for maintaining that motivation. Let your passion for books be your guide, and use whatever method suits you best - a spreadsheet, calendar, app, or a simple notebook - to record the titles and authors of each book you conquer. Witnessing the number of books you have devoured grow day by day will fill you with a sense of accomplishment and satisfaction, encouraging you to continue your journey towards bookish greatness!

In conclusion, achieving the goal of reading 100 books in a year is not only attainable but also an extraordinary feat that requires unwavering dedication and effort. To make this dream a reality, you must have a well-planned reading strategy and allocate time specifically for reading. Choose literature that captivates your imagination and feeds your soul and never forget to monitor your progress and stay motivated. You can join a literary group or take part in virtual reading challenges to keep your inspiration high. With discipline and persistence as your allies, reaching your target of reading 100 books within a year is within your grasp. So, turn the pages, and let the magic of books take you on a journey to achieve greatness!

7.3 5 Ways to get the most out of any book

You know that reading is an important part of personal and professional development. It is a great way to gain knowledge, gain new perspectives, and enhance critical thinking skills. However, reading is not just about flipping through pages and getting to the end of a book.

To get truly benefit from reading, it is important to learn how to read effectively. I share here the five ways to get the most out of any book. These techniques help you read effectively, keep information, and apply the concepts you learn in your daily life. Whether you're reading for pleasure or for personal or professional development, these tips will help you get the most out of your reading experience and will help you become a more effective reader. So, dive in and discover how to get the most out of your reading.

1. Read each chapter twice before going to the next one.

To maximize your learning and comprehension while reading, it is advisable to read each chapter twice before moving on to the next one. This technique allows you to grasp the concepts and ideas presented in the chapter, as well as keep the information for longer periods. To maximize your learning and comprehension, read each chapter twice before moving on to the next one to identify key points and nuances that may have been missed during the initial read.

Repetition can help reinforce understanding and improve your ability to recall information. Incorporating this practice into your reading routine can ultimately enhance your overall learning experience and make the most out of your reading.

2. As you read, stop frequently to ask yourself how you can apply each suggestion.

Simply reading material is not enough. You should stop frequently and ask yourself how each suggestion can be applied in practical terms in order to benefit from the material. This will help you keep the information and also develop a deeper understanding of the content. This practice can be useful when reading material related to your profession or industry, as it can lead to new ideas and approaches that can be implemented in your work. By taking a proactive approach to reading, you can get the most out of the information you consume and apply it effectively in your professional life.

3. Underscore each important idea.

It is essential to underscore each important idea while reading to ensure that you get the most out of the material. Whether you are reading for pleasure or studying for an exam, highlighting key points can help with comprehension and retention. This technique allows for easy reference when reviewing the material later. It can aid in identifying recurring themes or concepts. By underscoring critical ideas, you can effectively summarize the material and gain a deeper understanding of its content. In conclusion, adopting this practice can significantly enhance your reading experience and optimize your ability to retain valuable information.

4. Apply learning to solve your daily problems.

Using what you learn to solve problems you face is a good way to grow and get closer to reaching your goals. When you read, you can learn a lot, but it is important to take that information and use it to solve real-life problems. This makes you more involved in what you are reading and helps you think about how to use it to improve your life.

Doing this can help you be more happy in everything you do.

5. Note what lessons you have learned for the future.

When engaging in reading, it is important to note the lessons learned so that you can apply them in the future. By reflecting on the key takeaways and insights gained from the material, you can ensure that you get the most out of your reading experience. This practice not only helps you retain the information better but also enables you to put it into action to improve your personal and professional lives. By keeping a record of the lessons learned, you can also easily refer to them in the future, creating a valuable resource for your personal development journey. Therefore, it is crucial to make a habit of noting down the lessons learned to maximize the impact of your reading.

In conclusion, reading is truly essential to starting a new life. By reading, you open yourselves up to new ideas, knowledge, and perspectives that can help you grow and evolve as individuals. Whether it is through fiction or non-fiction, reading has the power to broaden your horizons, challenge your beliefs, and inspire you to pursue your dreams. So, if you're looking to embark on a new journey in life, make reading a part of that journey. It might just be the catalyst you need to turn your dreams into reality.

Key Takeaways - 7

1. Whether you read self-help books or stories, it can teach you new things and give you fresh ideas.

2. The top eight reasons for reading books are:

2.1. It improves concentration and focus
2.2. It increases knowledge and vocabulary
2.3. It enhances creativity and imagination
2.4. It develops analytical skills
2.5. It improves communication skills
2.6. It helps to build strong relationships.
2.7. It creates a sense of empathy
2.8. It boosts self-confidence and self-esteem

3. Reading 100 books in a year may seem difficult at first, but with the right mindset and resources, anyone can achieve this feat and reap the benefits.

4. To get truly benefit from reading, it is important to learn how to read effectively.

5. To maximize your learning and comprehension while reading, it is advisable to read each chapter twice before moving on to the next one.

6. When you read, you can learn a lot, but it is important to take that information and use it to solve real-life problems.

7. In conclusion, reading is truly essential to starting a new life.

Chapter 8: T=Teach What You Know

"Discover yourself, otherwise you have to depend on other people's opinions who don't know themselves."

- Osho

Teaching is an essential tool that serves as a catalyst to start a new life. It provides knowledge and shapes the character of an individual. Teaching helps to impart wisdom, instill good values, and promote critical thinking skills. In today's world, education has become a fundamental right, and teaching plays a vital role in ensuring that every individual has access to it. The power of teaching lies in its ability to change lives, inspire passion, and create a brighter future for generations to come.

If you are an excellent teacher, it means you are not only an educator but also a mentor, guide, and role model. You have the power to influence individuals in a way that no one else can. It is through your guidance and support that individuals can build their confidence, discover their passion, and develop the skills to lead a successful life. Whether it is in a physical mode or online, you can feel the impact of a great educator throughout a lifetime.

8.1 Why should you teach?

Teaching what I learn has been a wonderful opportunity for me to continue on my journey of helping individuals grow and reach their full potential. It is a truly rewarding act that demands passion, dedication, and a love for learning. I prefer to teach because I believe in making a difference in individuals' lives. It's a journey that requires hard work, unwavering commitment, and perseverance. I am motivated every day by the opportunity to inspire and guide individuals towards success.

If you want to start your new life, you must go for teaching. This does not mean that you choose a teaching career, it means whatever opportunities you get, teach others because that is needed for you and others. However, I share here the *top eight reasons* to go for teaching.

1. To pass on knowledge

Teaching ignites the flames of knowledge within the minds of any individuals. It fills you with a sense of duty to impart your wisdom to others, so they may go forth and achieve greater things. Through teaching, you have the privilege of unlocking the limitless potential of young minds and sow the seeds of lifelong learning. Teaching blossom individuals into knowledgeable one and empowers to change the world. The satisfaction of witnessing such things is indescribable.

2. To inspire the next generation

Teaching lets you inspire and help prepare the next generations for the future. Remember, education is super important for having a successful life. Try to make learning fun and interesting so that your surrounding people can be ready for their future.

It is also fun to keep learning about new things so that you can teach others about the world.

3. To help individuals reach their potential

Teaching can help individuals do their very best. You can make them to feel energized to take on a challenge and strive for their best. If you give them what they need to learn and grow, you will feel proud when you see them achieve their goals. You also ensure for them, it is important to take charge of their own learning and not be afraid to try new things. In this way, if you give individuals what they need to succeed through your teaching, they will be successful in everything they do.

4. To make a difference in life

Teaching is very rewarding because it always provides an opportunity to learn and grow. It improves you and helps you to contribute a major role in the success of other individuals. By teaching, you help others to achieve their life goals and understand more about the world. Is it not a special feeling to know that you have made a difference in someone's life?

5. To have a positive impact on society

Teaching has the power to change the world. Every lesson you impart to your surrounding people is a chance to spark their curiosity and inspire them to take action. If you teach someone, you are guiding them towards a future filled with endless opportunities by equipping them with the knowledge, skills, and values they need to create genuine change in their communities.

It is your purpose to instill in them a sense of motivation, to help them unlock their potential, and to encourage them to make a difference in the world. Make your aim at nurturing not just minds, but also hearts, and this helps individuals to be compassionate, empathetic, and active members of society.

6. To foster creativity and critical thinking

The power of critical and creative thinking is immeasurable in today's society. When you teach, you inspire individuals to develop such essential skills. Teaching imparts knowledge and inspires how to think, analyze, and create. Through the art of critical thinking, you can assess ideas and facts, as well as form your own opinions. By harnessing your creativity, you learn to be innovative, problem-solvers, and game-changers. If you can empower individuals with these tools, you are setting them up for success in navigating and thriving in a rapidly evolving world.

7. To build character and self-confidence

Teaching is a powerful way to help young minds soar. Make your mission to create a nurturing space where your surrounding people can thrive and develop into confident, resilient individuals. Your goal of teaching is to empower all individuals to explore their passions, find their unique voice, and cultivate a strong sense of self. Strive to instill in them the courage to embrace challenges as opportunities to grow and to take bold actions to achieve their dreams. With every lesson, activity, and conversation, you lay the foundation for a future where they are unstoppable in their pursuit of excellence.

8. To make learning fun and engaging

I believe that learning should be enjoyable and captivating. You should establish an atmosphere where individuals can investigate new subjects and concepts with excitement while discovering meaningful and entertaining ways to learn about the world. Captivating teaching enhances individuals' self-assurance and enthusiasm in learning.

Remember, teaching allows you to share knowledge, motivate and inspire individuals, and positively impact their lives. Not only does it offer personal growth and professional development, but it also provides the satisfaction of knowing that you are helping to shape the future leaders. Make it well worth it.

8.2 How will you teach?

In today's world, knowledge is power. As you strive to succeed, you need to ensure that you are using your knowledge to your full potential. One of the best ways to do this is to share your knowledge, skills, and expertise with others. Teaching what you know is an invaluable way to help those around you while also helping yourselves. Whether you are an entrepreneur, a student, or a professional, teaching what you know can benefit everyone involved.

Teaching what you know can help others. It can give others the skills and knowledge they need to succeed, and can also help them develop their own expertise. Teaching can also bring a sense of satisfaction, as it gives you the opportunity to share your knowledge and help those around you.

It can also be beneficial for your own personal growth, as teaching can help to expand your understanding and knowledge even further.

How will you teach?

Here are *seven important steps* to do that:

1. Identify what you know and are passionate about

To teach what you know, the first step is to identify what you know and are passionate about. Consider your hobbies, interests, and life experiences. Think about how you can use your knowledge to help others. Are you an expert on a particular subject? Do you have a unique skill set? How can you use your knowledge to help others? Once you have identified what you know and are passionate about, you can develop a plan for teaching it to others.

2. Research to stay up to date on the topics

Researching the topic you are teaching is essential to staying up to date on the subject. Not only will this help you stay on top of the latest trends and developments, but it will also help you create engaging, current content to use in your lessons. Reading books and articles can help you do research. Besides, attending conferences and seminars, and engaging in online conversations with other experts in the field are also good ways to do that. Keeping in contact with those who are currently working in the field will help you stay informed about any changes that have been made and any recent developments that have taken place.

3. Identify your target audience

To teach what you know, the most important step is to identify your target audience. Whom are you trying to reach with your message? Whom do you want to learn from you? Knowing your target audience will help you design the right message for them. Consider the demographics of your audience, such as age, gender, and location. You should also consider their interests and level of knowledge on the topic you are teaching. This will help you create a message that resonates with them and encourages them to take action.

4. Consider what your audience needs

The fourth step when teaching what you know is to consider what your audience needs. It is important to remember that the goal of teaching is to provide value to your audience, not just impart your own knowledge. Therefore, you need to think about what your audience needs to know and structure your teaching approach to that. You should also consider the level of knowledge your audience has to determine the best way to explain your concepts. If your audience is a beginner, you may need to provide more detail and use a simpler language. If your audience is already familiar with the topic, you can be more concise and direct. Taking the time to understand your audience's needs is essential for successful teaching.

5. Develop a plan for teaching

Before beginning to teach, it is important to create a plan for how you will teach. This plan should include what topics you will cover, how you will teach them, and how long your course will be. You should consider what materials you would need and determine how you will access them. Creating a plan also helps you to stay organized and on track while teaching. It is also important to consider who your target audience is and tailor your plan accordingly. By creating a plan for teaching, you can ensure that your course is effective and engaging for your learners.

6. Find an appropriate platform

After deciding what you want to teach and setting your goals, find an appropriate platform for teaching. Depending on your goals, you can create a course and sell it in various marketplaces, or you could create content free on a platform like YouTube or a blog. You can also opt for interactive learning sessions on video conferencing programs like Zoom or Google Hangouts. No matter which platform you choose, it is important to make sure it provides the features and services you need to teach effectively.

7. Practice your teaching skills

Teaching what you know is a great way to share your knowledge with others. In addition, the best way to become an outstanding teacher is to practice your skills. Whether it is preparing lesson plans, developing activities, or delivering lectures, the more you practice, the more confident and competent you will become as a teacher. Take advantage of every opportunity you can to practice your teaching skills, whether it is a workshop, an in-class assignment, or a full-time teaching position.

Moreover, do not forget to ask for feedback from those who have experienced your teaching—they can provide invaluable insight into how to improve your skills. With practice, you will be able to teach what you know with ease.

Ultimately, teaching what you know can be an incredibly rewarding experience, both personally and professionally. It not only helps build valuable skills, but also can provide you with the opportunity to share your knowledge and expertise with others. Whether you choose to teach in a classroom setting or online, you will be able to gain valuable insights and perspective from your learners, which can help you grow and develop both professionally and personally. Therefore, if you have a skill or expertise that you would like to share with others, teaching what you know can be a great way to do it.

Key Takeaways - 8

1. Teaching is an essential tool that serves as a catalyst to start a new life.

2. If you are an excellent teacher, it means you are not only an educator but also a mentor, guide, and role model.

3. Why should you teach?

3.1. To pass on knowledge
3.2. To inspire the next generation
3.3. To help individuals reach their potential
3.4. To make a difference in life
3.5. To have a positive impact on society
3.6. To foster creativity and critical thinking
3.7. To build character and self-confidence
3.8. To make learning fun and engaging

4. How will you teach?

1. Identify what you know and are passionate about
2. Research to stay up to date on the topics
3. Identify your target audience
4. Consider what your audience needs
5. Develop a plan for teaching
6. Find an appropriate platform
7. Practice your teaching skills

5. Ultimately, teaching what you know can be an incredibly rewarding experience, both personally and professionally.

CONCLUSION

****

"Believe you can and you are halfway there."

- *Theodore Roosevelt*

As you come to the end of this book, let you not forget the power of simplicity.

You must not let indecision and self-doubt hold you back from achieving your dreams. Instead, let you take care of your health by nourishing it with healthy food, getting enough rest, and staying active.

Remember, action is the key to unlocking your full potential and learning new skills. Let you embrace the joy of knowledge and share it with others, for in doing so; you inspire and enrich your community. By adopting these steps, you can create a life of purpose, fulfillment, and vitality.

Take the first step towards a healthier and happier life today.

START your new life!

Acknowledgment

To **God** who is the Power behind existence.

To **my parents** who inspire me to take challenges in life and make me understand the meaning and importance of freedom.

To all my **friends** and **relatives** who directly and indirectly help me to excel in every sphere of life.

Gratitude: Request to Readers

Please accept my gratitude for reading My Books.

Every book teaches us something new.

I need your input to make the next version of this book and my future books even better.

If you love reading this book, I request you to head over to Amazon or wherever you purchased this book to leave an honest and helpful review for me so that I can know what you thought of the book!

I really appreciate all of your feedback, and I love hearing what you have to say.

Do not forget. Every review means lots to me*!*

Just four easy steps to do:

1. Go to the book page (or just search for START Your New Life on Amazon).
2. Click on write a customer review in the Customer Reviews section.
3. Click Submit.
4. Check if your review is published.

I thank you endlessly.

With love and gratitude,

Prabin Sharma

About the Author

Prabin Sharma is the bestseller author of the books (1) *THE WAY I LEARN* (2) *NEW YEAR 21* (3) *Promotion Secrets You Never Knew* (4) *Make Your Life Blissful.* And (5) *Be a STAR Manager.*

START Your New Life is his sixth book in English. He is a blogger, memoirist, storyteller, experienced Senior Banker, public speaker, mentor, personal growth and productivity expert.

He writes because he loves to share his knowledge and experiences with the world and to inspire individuals to take immense actions. He enjoys writing on personal growths, career accelerations, financial awareness, Self-help, productivity and purpose-driven life. He also loves writing short stories, memoirs, poems and fictions.

He believes and advocates the concept of *'I am because we are'*. The symbiotic relationship is the reason for our existence.

He is the father of two divine daughters and a husband of a goddess wife. He enjoys traveling, reading, watching movies, and listening to instrumental music.

Upcoming Book of the Author

Are you married or going to marry?

Do you want to make your marriage work?

Is there mutual understanding between you and your life partner?

Do you want to uncover inner happiness in your married life?

Do you have any strategies for lasting love?

Craft a Happy Marriage is a comprehensive guide for couples looking to strengthen and nurture their relationship.

This book dives deep into the power of love and how to use it to create a strong, fulfilling relationship. You will learn how to communicate effectively, practice empathy and understanding, and find harmony in your life together.

With a combination of practical tips and thoughtful advice, this book provides real-world strategies to help couples:

♥ Build a strong bond,
♥ Develop meaningful communication,
♥ Strengthen conflict resolution, and
♥ Increase understanding and trust.

It also covers topics such as: -

◆ The importance of friendship,
◆ Setting goals,
◆ Creating a shared vision, and
◆ Dealing with life's challenges like parenting, finances, and health.

By using the book's advice, couples can learn to create an honest and deep bond, one that will help them through both the good and the difficult times. Couples will also learn to appreciate each other more and to respect each other's needs and wishes.

Also By the Author

Do you desire to take control of your life?

Do you know your purpose in life?

Do you know how to develop your vision and overcome obstacles?

Do you want to make your life blissful?

The Way I Learn helps you to discover your potential through life lessons from the real-life events of my life and my challenges, struggles, pains, problems, fears, and continuous endeavors to grow and desire to accomplish what I deserved.

This memoir takes you on the rollercoaster of twists and turns, from facing the worst-case life situations to achieving a better life-style, and suggests resolutions to various conflicts in your life. It culls the essence of life for you. Life always teaches you. This book shares all such important life lessons.

Do you follow your heart?

Do you procrastinate often to build the best healthy habits?

Do you desire to achieve what you want from your life?

Do you doubt you will enjoy your future?

Are you still struggling to set goals?

It does not matter much whether your answer is yes or no. What matters is your desire to learn the success formula, your perseverance and your consistency. All individuals dream of accomplishments, wisdom, holistic growth and abundance in their life, but very few can only achieve all of them.

Do you want to know its secrets?

Years come and go. You make resolutions to transform your life every year, but you can't remain consistent in sticking to your resolutions and miss accomplishing your personal and professional goals. Every year remains the same – a common and ordinary year.

Do you feel guilty about that?

You will answer in affirmation but I guarantee you that it is neither your fault nor your bad luck. What inhibits your growth is not circumstances but the lack of a clear understanding of your inner strengths and your true potentials. The ineffective process or steps you follow to achieve your heart's yearning deliver your failures, because those so-called effective strategies that you read, listen, or watch are unpredictable, perplexing, demanding, and depressing.

If your steps are not in the right direction, you will never reach the desired destination. *Your goals are your destination.* Finding the right direction and to follow it until you reach your dream goals demand wisdom. How will you attain wisdom and the right direction for attaining your goals?

This book *NEW YEAR 21: 8 Effective Steps to Get Your Heart's Desire, Improve Health, Build Best Habits and Achieve Life Goals* is full of wisdom and practical experiences that will show you the right direction and also share insights on a well-established and time tasted 8-Step process to ensure getting your heart's desire, improving health (both the physical and the mental one), building the best habits and achieving your life goals.

This book will help you keep you going in your chosen direction while staying open to even greater possibilities. You will get clarity on your power, passion, and purpose. This book will show you a definitive path to success, self-awareness, and self-mastery so that you can create your desired future.

Inside this book, you will learn how to have a more positive impact on your lives and prepare yourself for the success you always desire and deserve. You will also learn how to build good habits and achieve remarkable goals.

This book will answer all your queries using and explaining the NEW YEAR 21 formula.

Are you ready to know and use the NEW YEAR 21 formula?

Remember, the ability to change lies within you.

If you are ready to take steps forward, you will reach your destination. No external forces, but your inner voices and determination make you healthy, wealthy, successful, and an achiever.

Johann Wolfgang von Goethe once said, *"What is not started today is never finished tomorrow."*

Are you ready to start today?

Read this book today to discover your winning habits for creating the success you want, achieving all your goals, building the health you desire, and the wealth you deserve.

Dare to dream!

You reach at the complete guidebook to Online Written Examinations, Group Discussions and Personal Interviews for your Promotions.

Get yourself listed in the final merit selection list.

Are you preparing for your promotion examinations?

Are you planning to move up in your career ladder?

You will know the study acceleration formula in this book if you study for written tests and face problems with retention of relevant information and facts.

You will get a roadmap for sure success in Group Discussions if you prepare for Group Discussions and face the problems of taking initiatives, leads and low confidences.

You will learn the proven plan to excel and enjoy your upcoming Personal Interviews if you hate appearing in Personal Interviews, feel bored and think those are obstacles in your career growth.

Who will not want to build a powerful Promotion Plan in 7 days?

You will learn to build your powerful Promotion Plan in 7 days or fewer by reading this book.

In this comprehensive unconventional book, you will also learn Promotion Secrets and, you will master the following essential aspects of the promotions:

* 9 Study Skills and Techniques
* 7 Group Discussions secrets
* 10 Personal Interview secrets
* Promotion Mindset
* Review and Revision plans
* Goal Setting in Career Growth
* 7 things your boss expects from you to consider your promotion.

And you will also benefit from case studies and bonuses topics on:

* Mental Skills like Emotional Intelligence, Attitude and Confidence, etc.

* Time and stress management before, during, and after the Promotion Process.

* Self-Motivation for studying and ensuring success

* Confidence to handle and work under pressure.

If you desire to advance in your career, pick up your copy of this book.

How can one prepare oneself to fight successfully against the problems?

What are the tools to discover and invent solutions to all problems?

Whether solutions lie in our minds or outside?

This book, **Make Your Life Blissful** has answers to such questions. It is all about your problems of life, defining them, finding their solutions, and tools or habits to sharpen fast and effective results, which ultimately make your life blissful.

The **purpose** of this book is:

- To discuss and detect the single and core problem of your life that hinders happiness and peaceful life.

- To enlighten you to invent the solutions for your core problem.

- To allow you to explore the 5 powerful habits (I call them GAMES) to listen to your inner voices.

- You will also learn about building blissful habits and their importance in achieving the purpose of life, along with solving the problems.

- You will know the panacea for your all pains and problems.

- To enable you to choose the right voice over inner noises.

- To help you make your life blissful and free from suffering.

★ This book contains gems of age-old wisdom and I apply everything written here and always get my desired and productive outcomes still now. If it works for me, it should also work for you.

★ You will agree with me it is problems in your life that make your blessed life as suffering. If you can eliminate or reduce the negative impacts of problems of life to some extent, you can enjoy your desired life and make your life blissful.

★ This book will guide you to solve your all problems systematically.

Excited?

I have also incorporated some practical **Mental Workouts** to enable you to explore your hidden potential and engage you to do such activities that lead you to reveal the solution to your root problem of life.

Let us begin together on the exciting journey of problem-solving adventures and making your life BLISSFUL.

HOW OFTEN DO YOU WANT TO CRY?

DO YOU LACK QUALITY TIME IN YOUR LIFE?

IS THIS THE TIME TO CHANGE YOUR ATTITUDES?

CAN YOU ENJOY YOURSELF AT WORK AND IN LIFE?

If you are a working professional or an employee, you must have experienced several stresses in your life. Your productivity and creativity always demand more time. Your life and work are not in a state of equilibrium. You may find yourself at sea. You often feel frustrated because of conflicts created because of a mixup of professional relationships with personal relationships.

If you resonate with such types of problems, this book, *Be a STAR Manager***: How To Manage Stress, Double Your Time, Change Attitudes And Build Relationships at Work And in Life**, is for you. This book provides you with useful content that covers the following essential topics and helps you to be an effective individual at work and in life:

o   Awareness about your time and its effective utilization.
o   Understanding of saying - Work is worship.
o   Details information about your key problems.
o   Knowledge about Signs of stress, reasons for increasing stress, and the Impact of stress in your life.
o   Analysis of Customers' time-work expectations
o   Several useful Time management tips
o   Aspects of Attitude Management
o   Insights on Four Life stages
o   Practical tips for increasing work efficiency and many more interesting topics.

This book answers questions like:

✓   Why should you be happy?
✓   How to enjoy your work?
✓   What are stress and its type?
✓   How to reduce stress?
✓   How to double your available time?
✓   What are the four pillars of relationship management? Etc.

After reading this book, you will equip yourself to be a STAR manager. Who is the STAR manager? This book defines a STAR manager as an individual who can manage stresses, time, attitude, and relationships effectively.

Are you ready to be a STAR manager?

If you desire to Manage Stress, Double Your Time, Change Attitudes and Build Relationships at work and in life, pick up your copy of this book.

Printed in Great Britain
by Amazon

41262663R00076